Streets and Lanes
of Midland Red

Malcolm Keeley
and Roger Torode
on behalf of Transport Museum Wythall and The Bus Archive

Capital Transport

Above: D5B 3821 is approaching the top end of Kidderminster's High Street on its way into the town centre. The bus has come from Birmingham and will be terminating at Bewdley. Most of these buildings were demolished for a typical 1960s shopping precinct and the area is now fully pedestrianised. *Roger Torode collection*

Front cover: A Black Country scene with FEDDs 2254 and 2219, and a pair of GD6s, outside Cradley Heath railway station. The area alongside the railway was later redeveloped by the West Midlands Passenger Transport Executive as a bus station and car park, providing an excellent interchange that is still in use. *Peter Mitchell*

Back cover top: Birmingham's New Street was an important terminus for Midland Red services for many years. Wartime Daimler CWA6 2512 with Weymann body rebuilt by Willowbrook loads in New Street, followed by two D5s. The building behind 2512 is named King Edward House, a reminder of the old school that used to stand on this site until the 1930s. Littlewoods would soon invest in a new store on High Street. Midland Red provided two principal routes between Birmingham and Coleshill, dividing at Castle Bromwich - the 161 via Water Orton and the 168 via Bacons End. There were short workings, including the 171 to Water Orton seen here, a separate number discontinued in 1969. *G H F Atkins archive/ S J Butler collection*

Back cover bottom: Midland Red services could be very obscure, some running on only one day a week. S22 5901 batters its way through encroaching greenery on its way to Upton-on-Severn. *Peter Mitchell*

Title page: S17 5564 loads at the Royal Oak, Quarry Bank, in August 1968 with D9 4958 positioned to overtake. The D9 is on the long 138 service which took around 80 minutes to travel between Birmingham and Kingswinford, including serving another Royal Oak at Lapal. *Midland Red/ The Bus Archive*

First published 2020

ISBN 978 1 85414 448 5

Published by Capital Transport Publishing Ltd
www.capitaltransport.com

Printed by Parksons Graphics

Introduction

Bus service demand peaked in the years following World War Two. Midland Red's pre-war management at times seemed to regard double-deck buses as a last resort but the stated policy of the post-war General Manager, Donald Sinclair, was to obtain the maximum number of double-decker vehicles which road obstructions etc made it possible to operate and to ensure the whole of the Company's fleet would be of the maximum seating capacity permitted by the regulations. To meet that first objective, tree cutters ensured as many of its busy routes between towns could be operated by double-deckers. There was therefore a glorious period when you could see much of the Midlands from the upper deck seat of a Midland Red bus. You could go into a Midland Red enquiry office in Banbury and learn everything you wanted to know about getting to, say, Shrewsbury and the local bus services you may have needed at the destination. No computers, of course, but the information was there in paper form.

The writers are delighted to respond to an idea by Jim Whiting of Capital Transport to bring the Midland Red route network in all its wide variety back to life on the printed page and in particular pay tribute to the fine photography of the late Peter Mitchell. Other important sources have been the Transport Museum Wythall and The Bus Archive. We hope that you enjoy the results and will spare a thought for just how long the photographers may have waited to get the shots you see here. The writers confess that they are not familiar with all 7,000 route miles operated by the company. We often have been dependant on the photographer for the location details, checking where possible and being constantly amazed at how even the quietest places have changed in half a century.

Midland Red revived a prewar idea called the Day Anywhere ticket in the late 1950s. The more modern buses tended to work the flagship services so it was largely D7s, LD8s, D9s and S15s that wafted day trippers, commercial travellers and, of course, enthusiasts armed with Day Anywhere tickets to and fro across the Midlands. Some of the towns were on the point of changing hugely with, for example, large numbers of houses to be constructed in Tamworth and Redditch, absorbing people from Birmingham. A town called Telford was proposed that would change forever the lonely Wells Fargo feel of the X96 between Shrewsbury and Wolverhampton. The ability to get around by bus included the relatively depopulated magic lands to the west of the River Severn. This area still seems unchanged today although locals will no doubt provide a full list of 21st century impertinences to prove nothing and nowhere remain the same. Nevertheless it is perhaps there that one feels at any minute a D7 bursting with bank holiday trippers will pass in the opposite direction. Cue a melancholic work by Worcestershire's Edward Elgar.

The writers' nostalgia for a probably imaginary paradise lost must be the result of brainwashing over many years by Midland Red's publicity material. The company was very keen to fill vacant seats in the off-peak, tempting people out of the towns and cities to enjoy a taste of rural bliss. The rural reality was different for many, of course. Grandad Keeley moved at the beginning of the 20th century from Chipping Campden to the Great Western Railway in Birmingham – life on a steam railway being less onerous than working a quarry supplying the Cotswold stone that is so valued today. For the ultimate in romantic persuasiveness, Midland Red went into overdrive with its coach cruise promotions, for example leaving us convinced that every Scotsman wore a kilt and every Welsh woman boasted a pointy hat. For those interested in all aspects of Midland Red marketing and design, the writers covered the story in *Midland Red Style*, also published by Capital Transport.

'Magic lands to the west of the River Severn'. BMMO S17 5606 at Great Witley on 23 June 1971. *Peter Mitchell*

It is almost certainly not a coincidence that the peak of Midland Red's powers matched the maximum enthusiast interest in the company, encouraged by the giveaways such as photographs and the frequently updated fleet list, handily provided in the form of a pocket-sized booklet with pink card cover. How we looked forward to the next edition! This glorious time lasted little more than a decade as passenger numbers shrank in the 1960s and the new 36-feet long single-deckers, seating 50 or more, became adequate for many services – and soon disposed of the now hard-to-recruit conductors too.

A Day Anywhere ticket was an important investment of pocket money and the temptation was to cover as much mileage as possible. Boyhood energy meant conversations like 'Right, that's Ludlow done, let's find the X35!' or 'OK, we've got 20 minutes to do Hinckley garage then we must be back on the 658!' The days were very long but, as night fell, you were warmed by your nylon shirt and a pullover in the latest man-made fabric together producing, if only it could have been harnessed, enough electricity to power a trolleybus.

Cameras and film were another considerable investment so not surprisingly most of us played it safe and took our pictures in bus stations where a good result was most likely. A small number of photographers, however, moved beyond those hallowed portals to get images of Midland Red buses going about their business. Some trod the busy city streets while just a few must have invested a huge amount of time capturing rare images in the deepest rural lanes.

In addition to the photographers, the writers particularly thank Hugh Taylor, without whom the Peter Mitchell pictures would not have been available, Mike Jordan, Midland Red archivist at the Transport Museum Wythall, Bernard Davis at The Bus Archive, and the National Library of Wales. Special thanks to Ken Jubb for allowing access to his colour transparencies. Suppliers of information have been many and include Francis Bickerstaff, Alan Briggs, Paul Gray, Mike Greenwood, Peter Jaques, Lloyd Penfold and David Williams.

This is intended primarily as a picture album, although with plenty of information, but those wanting detailed histories of the company and its buses are already well-served by other books. For those whose knowledge is negligible, here are a few basic facts to help you.

The Birmingham & Midland Motor Omnibus Co Ltd – familiarly known as Midland Red - grew under British Electric Traction control to become England's biggest private bus company in the years between the two World Wars. The company was unusual in not having a General Manager at this time. The reins were jointly held in an uneasy partnership by Mr Shire, the Chief Engineer, and Mr Power, the Traffic Manager. An interesting by-product of the division of responsibilities was that drivers were regarded as quasi-engineers under Mr Shire while conductors fell under Mr Power, with quite different uniforms of brown and blue respectively. Midland Red was so large that, originally frustrated by what outside manufacturers could offer, it designed and built most of its own buses and coaches between 1923 and 1970. Mr Shire christened them SOS but refused to state the meaning of the initials. They may have meant 'Superior Omnibus Specification' but Shire was a proud man and the suspicion is they really stood for 'Shire's Own Specification'!

World War Two from 1939 meant the company's bus production was suspended and, by the time the conflict ended in 1945, the company was managed on more orthodox lines with the hugely talented Donald Sinclair installed as General Manager. Midland Red bus production resumed but Mr Sinclair took exception to the SOS badging which could be translated as the distress signal 'Save Our Souls'! Company-built buses and coaches operated under Mr Sinclair's watch carried the initials of the proper name of Midland Red and pre-war buses were rebadged with the new BMMO branding. Mr Sinclair retired at the end of 1966.

British Electric Traction sold its British bus companies to the state in 1968 causing Midland Red to become part of the resulting National Bus Company. Midland Red ceased building its own buses in 1970 so the vehicle stock in this book closes at the beginning of 1971 with the absorption of subsidiary company Stratford Blue and just before the NBC was to step up its influence.

Opposite top: The Priory Gatehouse, today commonly known as the Abbey Gateway, was the entry to the Benedictine Priory of Great Malvern. Parts of the structure date back to the 15th century, this face was 'restored' in the 1890s when the crenellations were added. Midland Red drivers eased their way through carefully, including the pilot of S8 3282 on 29 June 1962. Other motorists were not so careful and, not surprisingly, the road is now closed to traffic. Today it is the entrance to the Malvern Museum of Local History and it is hard to believe that underfloor-engine buses with their high floors ever squeezed through here. *Lyndon W Rowe*

Opposite: Great Malvern's gateway is even more extraordinary because the south side is quite different architecturally, having been widened in Tudor brick style around 1600, as seen in this shot of 1968 S23 5919. *Transport Museum Wythall*

Bus photography before the digital age

Mmm, got to get this right – this place is awkward to get to and the bus only runs every hour. This new camera has several speeds so at last I can get away from the bus stations. What exposure? Can't afford a light meter so I've got to guess – I've become pretty good at it. The sun is out but not fully. Should stop the picture being too stark but less light combined with the need for speed means less depth of field. These colour transparency films are so slow. 500th at f4 should do it.

Any minute now. Can't believe this, I've been on this rural footpath for 35 minutes and not seen a soul. Now there's a bloke wandering along, he's seen the camera and looks a bit surly about it. Bet he gets in the way or starts a conversation. Come on, bloke, the bus is due. There's a bit of luck, the bus is late and the pedestrian passes me with a brief glimpse of teeth like a burned-out fusebox. Probably phoning the local copper now.

The wind suddenly catches my face and I think I can hear a D9. That distinctive soft beat, mellow yet powerful – lovely! Can't see it yet but, sure enough, here it comes over the horizon. Blimey, he's late and he's shifting – the beat is urgent, a D9 can easily do fifty on this sort of road. Stupid boy, have I got time to change to 1000th at f2.8? Is the sun going in? Quick look over my shoulder, hopefully that cloud won't get to the sun before the D9 streaks by. No time to alter anything, get the background in as you've rehearsed for the last 35 minutes. Travelling at this speed, it's a good job this is more of a front-on shot than normal.

Almost subconsciously I note the conductor has set the blinds correctly, another stroke of luck but I hope the sun doesn't reflect off the glass. Through the viewfinder I can see the front seat passengers rising and dipping - the D9 has superb stability from side to side but that engine ahead of the front axle encourages the rubber suspension to nod, especially at this speed. Wow, this D9 is running on the governor, listening to the sound almost makes me forget to take the picture. Click and the D9 is gone, leaving a whirl of dust. Now two weeks' delay while I take the rest of the film, post it off to the film manufacturer and wait for the slides to come back.

S13 3957 waits for its chance to cross the A435 at Bransons Cross to reach Beoley on infrequent service 343 in July 1958. This scene has completely changed following widening of the A435 to dual carriageway. There is now an underpass for the junction but BMMO buses still regularly operate through here from the Transport Museum Wythall. *F W York/ Transport Museum Wythall*

A BRIEF GUIDE TO SERVICE NUMBERING

In April 1925, Midland Red renumbered its services into geographical groups. Despite leaving gaps, expansion was greater than anticipated, and in February 1928 the routes were again renumbered in geographical blocks but this time allowing for expansion right up to 999. The 1928 allocation of numbers was as follows:

100 upwards	Birmingham and Black Country
288 upwards	Kidderminster
318 upwards	Bromsgrove and Redditch
352 upwards	Worcester, Malvern and Evesham
422 upwards	Hereford
479 upwards	Banbury
513 upwards	Leamington and Stratford-upon-Avon
576 upwards	Rugby and Coventry
601 upwards	Leicester, Coalville and Ashby
725 upwards	Nuneaton
776 upwards	Atherstone and Tamworth
821 upwards	Rugeley, Cannock and Stafford
879 upwards	Wolverhampton
898 upwards	Oakengates and Wellington
926 upwards	Shrewsbury

Also from 1928, prefix letters for purely local services began to be introduced to conserve the reserved blocks of numbers. The prefix was the first letter of the city or town involved, and the accompanying service number did not exceed 99. Not all were new services, some were renumberings from the main series to make way for additional rural routes. These arrangements worked excellently, proving robust enough to meet the company's peak in the 1950s with only slight tweaking.

An X series became associated with the company's longer bus services. They were not traditionally limited stop but some included minimum fare sections to avoid longer distance passengers being crowded off by local riders. The X series also grew to include works, school, hospital, forces' leave services and holiday period services to popular scenic destinations. It was decided from 1966 to reserve the X prefix for true limited stop services, about to be rapidly expanded. Services not fitting the description were renumbered into the main series or, if works services, added to the A series, originally intended for Austin journeys in the Birmingham area.

Pre-war buses had stencil service numbers that would rattle in their boxes instead of the roller blinds that became familiar later. Although three figure service numbers were usual, only two stencils of each number were supplied with each vehicle and numbers like 111, 222 had to be avoided. The last pre-war buses finished at the end of 1960. Sutton Coldfield service revisions from 25 November 1961 introduced 111 and other triple identifications soon followed.

SON 2315, working a Shrewsbury local service, shows the destination boards and route number stencils used on the pre-war buses. The stencil numbers were almost indestructible but needed to be illuminated as seen here. 2315 is carrying luggage behind the front mudguard, possibly deliveries to a couple of village newsagents. An AD2 class AEC Regent is following.
PM Photography

British Electric Traction had many transport interests around the UK including the Kidderminster & Stourport electric tramway. The Allen Motor Omnibus Company introduced buses to compete with the trams so, in October 1913, BET took action to protect its interests in the area. Until the delivery of ten new buses, eight Daimlers were hired from Northern General Transport – another BET company – and are thought to have been diverted on their journey north from the manufacturers. One of the Daimlers, J 2547, is seen outside the Talbot Hotel in Chaddesley Corbett. Competition became severe as new motor bus services were developed from Kidderminster but agreement was reached with Allen in early 1914. A new company, Worcestershire Motor Transport, was formed on 22 July 1914 to combine the BET's Kidderminster and Worcester bus operations. The Talbot Hotel provided the backdrop for some Midland Red promotional pictures in the 1950s and, happily, this part of Chaddesley Corbett remains almost unchanged in appearance today. *Roger Torode collection*

The Five Ways, Four Oaks

This is Five Ways but not the better known business centre on the edge of Edgbaston – this one is in Four Oaks. 1914 Tilling-Stevens TS3 OA 4557 is working the Birmingham – Mere Green service via Wylde Green and Sutton, then numbered 18. Midland Red was now expanding rapidly, linking Birmingham with cities such as Coventry, Worcester and other nearby towns. *Roger Torode collection*

Opposite top: Commencing operations in 1905, the Birmingham and Midland Motor Omnibus Company from 1907 became an organisation without motor omnibuses, having reverted entirely to horses after problems with the new-fangled technology. Motor buses returned in 1912 and Mr Shire's choice of Tilling-Stevens petrol-electric chassis, with their absence of gears, made the transition from horse buses easier for drivers. The first thirteen were TTA1 models used on two services from central Birmingham, to Harborne and along Hagley Road to Bearwood. The latter's terminus on Sandon Road, near the Bear Hotel, is seen here, O 8206 loading outside a handy coffee shop with early opening. The next delivery, comprising TTA2 double-deckers, would introduce the MIDLAND fleet name. Potential disputes with Birmingham Corporation's transport department were solved by a non-competition agreement in 1914 involving, among other things, the sale of some buses to the Corporation, including O 8206. Importantly the agreement led to the great expansion of Midland Red throughout the towns and countryside of the Midlands. Initially O C Power, the dynamic Traffic Manager, declared an intention to connect up all the towns and villages within a radius of 30 miles of Birmingham. The agreement successfully lasted until the 1969 creation of the West Midlands Passenger Transport Executive overtook it. *Malcolm Keeley collection*

Opposite: The Kidderminster & Stourport tramway company started bus services to Bewdley and Cookley in 1913, these routes becoming part of Worcestershire Motor Transport the following year as described on page 8. However, the new company's fleet of Leylands was commandeered by the War Office on the outbreak of war later in 1914 so its services were taken over by BMMO using vehicles then surplus in Birmingham, and BMMO operated them from then on. This picture, dated 1914, is thought to show the first Midland Red bus to Bewdley with its crew and, on the right, J H Cooper, the proprietor of the George Hotel. After the initial purchases of double-deck buses, which were mostly sold to Birmingham Corporation under the 1914 agreement, the company began to standardise on single-deckers. O 9940 was one of the first batch of six delivered in 1913; their 27-seat bodies by Birch were the only single-deckers purchased new with rear entrances. *Roger Torode collection*

Above: Midland Red opened up country towns with the minimum of vehicles and manpower. Handbills were posted through letterboxes, advising that Midland Red buses would begin running the following day – to the disgust of proprietors of horse-drawn carrier carts plying to and from the towns, particularly on market days. Banbury's initial operations from 13 October 1919 used three buses on routes to Deddington, Hook Norton, Chipping Norton, Brackley, Byfield, and Shipston-on-Stour. The driver (on the left) of 1920 Tilling-Stevens OH 1224 was Mr William Webb whose experiences during World War One with the Army's Mechanical Transport section gave him engineering and driving expertise that was ideal for the infant Midland Red. Although primarily based at Banbury, Mr Webb helped open up services at Wolverhampton and Tamworth. He was later appointed as a driver suitable for private hires, becoming a well known personality in Banbury by the time of his retirement in 1960. *Transport Museum Wythall collection*

Opposite top: World War One (1914-8) assisted Midland Red's expansion because its Tillings were not favoured by the military. Growth away from Birmingham was encouraged by taking over services from companies that had run out of steam under the pressures of the war or whose buses had been requisitioned. In the former category was sister BET company North Warwickshire. Midland Red buses started to work what remained of its network of services out of Nuneaton and Tamworth from 1 February 1918. Bus crews were a male occupation at the beginning of the 20th century but World War One saw the temporary introduction of conductresses as seen here at Tamworth station. Females returned in World War Two; conductresses becoming a permanent feature. They were joined by a small number of female drivers, undeterred by heavy clutches and steering, the last not retiring until shortly before their general acceptance in the 1970s. The destination boards on 1914 Tilling-Stevens TS3 OA 4562 working the 63, an ex-North Warwickshire service, can be seen very clearly. Those on the front display the ultimate destinations of the bus, while the side boards show the service number and are primarily intended to advise the via points. *Transport Museum Wythall collection*

Opposite: Midland Red introduced its first longer distance services in 1921, to Weston-super-Mare and Llandudno. Midland Red was a landlocked bus company; Weston and Llandudno were the nearest bits of seaside! Standard single-deckers were used, in this case even lacking a luggage carrier on the roof. Bodies at this time were built to Midland Red's specification by several favoured coachbuilders; Tilling-Stevens OE 6187 dates from 1920 and shows the style of body introduced that year when the contracts were divided between Birmingham Railway Carriage & Wagon (BRCW) and Strachans. Passengers can anticipate more solid tyre luxury as OE 6187 waits for the scheduled departure time from the Highgate Hotel, Whitchurch in Shropshire. *Transport Museum Wythall collection*

BIRMINGHAM, FIVE WAYS.

Now this is the better-known Five Ways in Birmingham. A smartly dressed chap with crisp white collar and highly-polished shoes boards the Bewdley bus at Five Ways in a scene including two Birmingham Corporation trams on its service 34 in Islington Row, a steam traction engine from the direction of Broad Street, a motor lorry and a horse-drawn cart. The fountain in the middle is a gathering point for local people. OH 1227, a Tilling Stevens TS3 with Strachan & Brown 32 seat body, was new in 1920 and its use on this key service probably indicates the early years of its life. The Bewdley destination board partially covers another saying Kidderminster, perhaps for its return to base from Bewdley. In 1920, Birmingham to Kidderminster took an hour and 35 minutes.
Roger Torode collection

Midland Red's enquiry office in Birmingham's Bull Ring had its frontage liberally covered in enamel signs as seen here. The company had to give up this site in 1937, moving to more tastefully decorated premises, since demolished, in Worcester Street. The double-deckers were a brief revival of the concept, 56 being produced between 1922 and 1924 on Tilling-Stevens chassis converted to forward control. Chief Engineer Shire designed the bodies which were built by the company in its Carlyle Road, Birmingham workshops. They had front entrances, most unusual on double-deck buses at this time. They seated 29 downstairs and 22 on top. The low upper deck capacity is explained by the arrangement of the seats along the centre, facing sideways, with access by sunken gangways each side, thus allowing decent clearance along the centre gangway in the lower deck. The idea of the sunken gangways was to minimise overall height to counter the relatively high chassis, reducing the chances of passengers being battered by overhanging trees on country roads. The front Tilling is leaving for Coventry with the upper deck very well filled. *Transport Museum Wythall*

A selection of buses loading in Angel Place, Worcester. Bearwood, Leicester and Worcester received permanent allocations of the Tilling-Stevens forward entrance double-deckers although other garages would borrow them and in time gained them in small numbers on their allocations. The one nearest the camera carries the service number 125 which was allocated to the Birmingham - Malvern service under the renumbering of services in 1925, being further renumbered to the very familiar 144 in 1928. Double-deck buses soon fell out of favour again, being withdrawn in 1928-9, some of the bodies being rebuilt to single-deck and remounted on former char-a-banc chassis. The prominent single-deck bus, OA 4574, was a 1914 Tilling-Stevens TS3. *Transport Museum Wythall collection*

A minority of vehicles were built as char-a-bancs for tours and excursions and Midland Red offered to quote for parties of any size. This is a huge outing to Evesham organised by the Dudley & District Co-operative Society around 1926, requiring service buses to supplement the char-a-banc fleet. *Midland Red/ courtesy The Bus Archive*

The post-World War One competition generally used small, fast, lightweight buses often on foreign chassis, which ran proverbial rings around the Midland Red Tilling-Stevens vehicles. Chief Engineer Mr Shire was very aware of this shortcoming and, after bus manufacturers failed to meet his requirement for vehicles that combined the capacity of the Tillings with the nimbleness of the small 'opposition' buses, he took the historic decision that the Company would design and build its own buses and char-a-bancs, bearing the initials SOS. The 1923-5 vehicles were normal control but, following a 1925 prototype, forward control SOS vehicles entered production in 1926 with the FS (Forward Steering) model and further designs quickly followed. HA 3516 is a char-a-banc version of the FS, seen in Monument Road, Edgbaston, Birmingham, with Ladywood Road in the background. *Transport Museum Wythall collection*

This is a large private hire assembled in Pitcher Bank, Stafford with merrymakers setting off for Stratford-upon-Avon about 1925. All the 'charas' are normal control SOS Standards except E1843 which was an ex-North Warwickshire Tilling-Stevens TS3 chassis fitted with a Tillotson char-a-banc body in 1919. 'Charas', as they were popularly known, did not have a centre gangway, each row of seats being accessed by individual doors. The Tillings had doors on both sides but the SOS vehicles had nearside doors only. Early SOS chassis were also supplied to other operators in the British Electric Traction empire.
Midland Red/ courtesy The Bus Archive

Opposite top: Midland Red soon discovered that the driver needed to be with the passengers on touring coaches, not separated in his own cab, so the company reverted to normal control vehicles for coach cruises. Midland Red always used the best hotels, here 1928 QC class HA 3676, with 30-seat coachwork also built by the operator, waits for its customers to return. *Transport Museum Wythall, courtesy John Harris*

Opposite: This interesting picture is probably showing a delivery run in 1928 of four QL class vehicles from bodybuilder Brush of Loughborough. The first two are Midland Red HA 3732 with Northern General UP 563 following. They had consecutive SOS chassis numbers 640 and 641. Another Northern General is behind, that company would add 65 QLs to its fleet before the year was out. Another QL for Midland Red brings up the rear. Bodies built by outside coachbuilders for Midland Red and its associated companies were supplied without interior fittings, notably seats, which would be added at Carlyle Works. With the onset of the serious economic depression that started in 1929, coachbuilders demanded that this practice should end to protect work for their own employees. Midland Red retired HA 3732 in 1938 but Northern General ran UP 563 until 1945. 1928 would be the record year for SOS production with no less than 349 buses and 30 coaches of which around half were for the Midland Red fleet and the remainder for associated companies. *Transport Museum Wythall, courtesy John Harris*

MM class HA 5012 provides service 519 on Shipston-on-Stour's wide and impressive High Street during the 1930s. Midland Red and the then independent Stratford Blue had signed an agreement to reduce competition in the Stratford-upon-Avon area in June 1929, predating the regulation brought by the Road Traffic Act 1930. The Stratford – Newbold – Shipston-on-Stour road was shared under the agreement and, in 1935, Stratford Blue became a subsidiary of Midland Red. In 1949 Stratford Blue and City of Oxford Motor Services introduced a joint service, numbered 44, between their home towns via Shipston. The combined frequency of services between Stratford and Shipston may only have been roughly hourly but your bus could be supplied by no less than three British Electric Traction subsidiaries! After years of running buses to rather basic standards, Midland Red's 1929 M type introduced new levels of comfort. Indeed M stood for Madam, demonstrating the desire to encourage ladies to travel, especially in the off-peak, and the standard seating capacity for service buses for the next few years was reduced to 34. The M was immediately followed by this modified version, the MM, which had six-cylinder engines as most of the chassis were originally intended for long-distance coaches. *Richard Stevenson collection*

The subsequent IM Class (Improved Madam) took quality further. HA 6217, a 1931 IM4 with 34-seat body by Short to Midland Red design is seen on Halesowen Road, Old Hill, working service 232 to Blackheath. This was a short working of the 230 between Dudley and Blackheath, and the 231 between Cradley Heath and Blackheath. A Midland Red parcels agency is on the extreme left. In the distance is AHA 537, a 1935 DON which was one of the company's first diesel buses. *Roger Torode collection*

WILLS's
CIGARETTES
SOLD HERE

SMOKE
BLUE BELL
TOBACCO
COOL & MELLOW

232

HA 6217

MIDLAND

HALESOWEN RD. OLD HILL

The driver is waiting to depart opposite the Barley Mow in Solihull on 8 May 1949, a spot almost unrecognisable today as road widening and redevelopment as offices have taken heavy toll of the trees. The 1930 Road Traffic Act brought an end to the overloading of buses with unsafe numbers of standees. This encouraged the company to design its own rear entrance double-decker, the SOS REDD with six cylinder engines, of which around fifty were produced. An internal series of bus and coach identification numbers was adopted as fleet numbers and applied to the actual vehicles as World War Two drew to an end; HA 8016 is seen with its fleet number 1371. The REDD body order was split between four coachbuilders, that on 1371 being built by Eastern Counties. In 1947 it was reported that the fleet strength stood at 1483 of which 311 buses had each covered more than half a million miles. Three of the production REDD buses, 1375/7/81, had clocked up over 650,000 – 1375 approaching 700,000 miles, equivalent to 28 times round the planet! Not bad for vehicles built only 20 years after the reintroduction of motor buses. *J Cull/ The Bus Archive*

Opposite top: As part of the endeavour to improve passenger comfort from 1929, around 50 of the original SOS 'Standard' buses were given new bodies, the old ones being transferred to earlier Tillings. The coachbuilder was United which later evolved into the rather better known Eastern Coach Works. This view of rebodied HA 2455, driven by Joe Wain, may be at Billesdon terminus, near Leicester. *Transport Museum Wythall, courtesy Martin Wain*

Opposite: Victoria Road, Sutton Coldfield is the location of HA 8289, a 1932 IM4 class with 34-seat body by Brush, awaiting its next departure after working the 109 route around 1938. *R T Wilson/ Transport Museum Wythall*

The increasing emphasis on passenger comfort was accompanied by improved bus performance; six-cylinder engined vehicles like the IM6 model occupied an increasing proportion of new stock. This is a 1937 view of 1933 IM6 HA 8304 in Hales Street, Coventry, on its way to Leamington via Kenilworth.
Transport Museum Wythall collection

The Burton & Ashby Light Railway was a railway-owned tramway that, in classic railway fashion, trundled across fields and missed a lot of intermediate housing. This gave bus operators the chance to compete, Midland Red joining in to contribute to the final knock-out which occurred on 19 February 1926. Burton-on-Trent's Wetmore Park bus station was a most interesting place to spend time, being host to several operators. SOS IM4 1461 was one of the last four-cylinder buses built by the company and has the more rounded body style introduced later in 1933. It shares the bus station on 10 June 1950 with a Burlingham-bodied Daimler single-decker of Victoria Motorways of Woodville, preparing to serve the Measham area. *Roy Marshall/ The Bus Archive*

Midland Red introduced LRR service coaches and OLR touring coaches between 1933 and 1935. These were relegated to bus services during World War Two and never reverted to coach duties. The alterations to the OLRs were considerable, being converted from normal to forward control, allowing an increase in seating from 29 to 34. 1681 waits to depart for Birmingham in Load Street, Bewdley. *Roger Torode collection*

Angel Place was the main terminal for Midland Red country services until 1946. Congestion became critical and, in December 1945, Midland Red and Worcester Corporation met to see what could be done. It is to the credit of everybody involved at that most difficult time just after World War Two that a properly designed and equipped bus and coach station was provided in six months off Newport Street and officially opened on 15 July 1946. The bus station and its shelters were owned by Worcester Corporation. 1934 saw the beginning of a very important family of SOS buses built by the company. This was the ON (short for Onward) with short cab and engine compartment, permitting 38 seats. The first ONs were petrol engined but compression-ignition (diesel) propulsion was becoming popular. Midland Red decided to design its own SOS diesel engine but, while development of what became known as the SON class took place, many of the 1935 deliveries had AEC 7.7 diesels forming the DON class. Some ONs were fitted with SOS diesels in 1937-8 and reclassified CON (Converted ON). This early post-war shot shows OLR class 1689 on the left and four SONs with 1905 leading 2038 and 2314. A FEDD can also be seen. *Transport Museum Wythall collection*

Today only a coach station, Midland Red's huge bus garage in Digbeth, Birmingham used to run the most annual mileage and became very overcrowded. Temporary use of land in front of the garage reserved for widening of the road to dual carriageway was agreed with Birmingham Corporation. The English Electric bodies on the 1937-8 SONs remained largely original, indeed this bus looks new with its old style of company fleet name yet the date is 29 April 1951 and it carries post-war fleet number 2205. Birmingham City Transport's overhead wires for its Coventry Road trolleybuses are visible but motorbuses are about to take over. *Peter Mitchell*

Many CONs and DONs had their Short Brothers or Brush bodies heavily rebuilt between 1947 and 1952, extending their lives until 1955-7. Earlier rebuilds were by Midland Red's own Carlyle Works to this rather severe metal frame design with square window corners. 1935 DON 1703 is seen at the Wagon & Horses, Uppingham on 9 April 1955. This bus survives and awaits restoration at the Transport Museum Wythall. *Peter Mitchell*

Later rebuilds featured flush-mounted windows with rounded corners. After prototypes were produced by Carlyle, large numbers were handled by Nudd Bros or Hooton. Despite the size of the major body rebuilding programme undertaken on pre-war stock after World War Two, very few chassis exchanged bodies. One of the few was 1523, new in 1934, which had been converted from ON to CON with a Midland Red diesel engine in 1938. Its Short Bros body was considered beyond repair in 1950 and replaced by another Short body, rebuilt by Nudd, taken off 1615 which had not been favoured with conversion to diesel and was withdrawn from service in that year. This enabled 1523, seen here at Shrewsbury Bus Station on 21 September 1955, to continue in service until 1956. *Peter Mitchell*

Also on 21 September 1955 DON 1721 is leaving Shrewsbury bus station on Barker Street on the S12 service to Castle Fields. The body is one of those rebuilt by Nudd Bros in 1949-50. The longer bonnet of the DON with a compensating short window behind the entrance can be seen. *Peter Mitchell*

The conductor enjoys the sunshine before collecting all those fares on the 355 to Himbleton via Crowle on 17 September 1955. The 1948 timetable showed two return trips on Monday, Tuesday and Sunday (morning and afternoon), three on Wednesdays and Fridays, five on Saturdays, but nothing on Thursdays. Clearly a service for shoppers rather than commuters. The company's own 8 litre diesel engine was evolved in time for the 1936 production run; the modified design of bus being classified SON which remained standard until production was halted by World War Two. Many SONs also had their bodies rebuilt after heavy use during the war, including 1892 passing farmers' lorries on its way out of Worcester's Newport Street bus station. *Peter Mitchell*

The body of 1911 was rebuilt at Hooton but, in 1955, it was more radically transformed to join the small fleet of tree cutters, an important job given the priority to achieve double-deck operation wherever possible. In this form it was based at Hereford and was seen on 31 August 1959. *Ken Swallow*

A serviceman marches briskly past CON class 1626 at Pool Meadow bus station, Coventry. In the shelter a man prepares to light his roll-up. Also to be seen is a City of Coventry Transport wartime bus that has also undergone similar body rebuilding attention. *C Carter*

1939 SON 2299 with Brush body rebuilt by Nudd works a local service along Worcester Road, Malvern Link, by Cromwell Road. 18 September 1957 was evidently a fine sunny day and the Malvern Hills look gorgeous, as does the late 1930s Triumph Dolomite car behind. *Peter Mitchell*

When bus services around Kidderminster settled down after competition in 1914, the Stourport route provided a service on the east side of the River Stour via Wilden, later extended to Astley Cross. This avoided competition with the BET trams which served the main road but progress meant that these were replaced by Midland Red buses in 1928. 2322 stands at the Post Office stop in Exchange Street, Kidderminster, on 21 September 1955, waiting to depart on the 313 to Astley Cross via Kidderminster Station, Wilden and Stourport. It is a 1939 SON with Nudd-rebuilt Brush body. Behind is FEDD 2131 on local service K6 to Greenhill, with the classic Old Judge Tea advert typical of these buses. In the background a D5B has arrived on the 133 from Stourport via the main road, and loads for Birmingham at the shelters alongside the Town Hall. *Peter Mitchell*

The double-deck equivalent of the ON class was the FEDD (Front Entrance Double-Decker). Again the earlier examples were petrol-engined but the 135 BHA-registered buses with metal-frame Metro-Cammell bodies were highly regarded and all were converted to diesel between 1942 and 1947. The introduction of this large fleet of bright red FEDD double-deckers, so very different in style from the blue rear-entrance trams and buses provided by Birmingham Corporation for its city services, must have had a considerable impact on the streets of Brum. This view shows a recently delivered Metro-Cammell bodied FEDD, BHA 361, around 1936. New Street looks very handsome but King Edward's School has moved to Edgbaston and demolition of the fine secular Gothic buildings dating from 1838 is taking place on the right. The Luftwaffe would deal with most of the remainder during World War Two. The 140 route via Blackheath to Dudley was one of many commencing in Station Street, Birmingham, and then picking up at this stop in New Street. Just look at the number of services calling here! Demand for Midland Red services continued to grow and the Hagley Road services were transferred to Navigation Street in 1950, the 140 being one of several moved again the following year, this time to Paradise Street. *Midland Red*

BUSES LOAD HERE FOR
BEARWOOD. BLACKHEATH.
BRIDGENORTH. BRIERLEY HILL.
BRISTNALL FIELDS. CHURCH STRETTON.
CLENT. DUDLEY. GORNAL WOOD.
HALESOWEN. KIDDERMINSTER. KINVER.
LANGLEY. LONDONDERRY. LUDLOW.
OLDBURY. ROMSLEY. SHREWSBURY.
STAFFORD. STOURBRIDGE.
WARLEY. WELLINGTON.
WOLVERHAMPTON. WOODGATE.

BENJAMIN PEARSON
DEMOLITIONS LTD.
ALBERT STREET & MOOR STREET
PHONE MID 5639.

MIDLAND RED MOTOR SERV

BUSES LEAVE AS FOLLO   BUSES LEAVE AS FOLLO

1936 FEDD/ Metro-Cammell 1816 is waiting to depart Worcester's Newport Street bus station on the 315 to Stourbridge via Kidderminster, displaying a not uncommon method of achieving two lines of destination on a single-line display! 1816 ran until 1953. *Roger Torode collection*

FEDD/Metro-Cammell 1836 in post-war condition outside the company garage in Church Road, Redditch, on 4 July 1953. *Peter Mitchell*

Midland Red purchased on 30 April 1930 Black & White Motorways Ltd of Cheltenham, one of the principal operators of long distance coach services. Black & White retained its separate identity, however, and its control was shared with two other companies, Bristol Tramways and City of Oxford Motor Services. 1 July 1934 saw a major step towards a nationwide, co-ordinated, coach network, with partners pooling specified services and operating them as an indivisible whole, eliminating wasteful competition. This was 'Associated Motorways', in which Midland Red was an important partner. The focal point was the Black & White coach station at Cheltenham where coaches connected and passengers interchanged. The last new petrol-engine vehicles built by the company were 50 SLR class luxury coaches, new in 1937. These were fitted with more economical Leyland E181 diesel engines upon refurbishment after World War Two. As old coaches fell due for replacement, Midland Red would loan some to Black & White. The latter usually applied temporary fleet numbers hence the tiny MR8 being carried by SLR 2006 at Cheltenham, accompanied by an ONC at its side and another SLR to the rear. *Ken Swallow*

Midland Red's first diesel-engine coaches were the 25 ONC vehicles of 1939 of which this one was numerically the first. Cheltenham Coach Station was a sea of colours at busy times, with Black & White, Red & White (actually red and cream), Yelloway, Ribble, and many others, but Midland Red's red and black livery always stood out smartly. 2269 does not state its destination on 29 May 1953 but is probably returning to Birmingham with the C3 behind. *Ken Swallow*

Further FEDDs were built in 1938-9 in three batches of 50. Brush built the bodies to a design that arguably lacked the period appeal of the earlier FEDDs. The Brush bodies all needed major rebuilding, mostly carried out in 1950-1, with flush-glazed windows and sliding vents – sometimes on the lower deck only. Use of the B prefix for a handful of Bromsgrove local services began on 1 September 1952. FEDD 2139 is working the B25 along The Strand, Bromsgrove on 21 September 1955. *Peter Mitchell*

Opposite top: FEDD 2129 is turning from Vicar Street into High Street, Kidderminster, setting off to Wolverhampton via Stourbridge. The policeman in his pulpit was a well-known feature of Kidderminster town centre until the pulpit was demolished in 1962 as part of a one-way system that made it unnecessary. According to legend, Traffic Manager O C Power used to slip the policeman five bob from time to time to ensure Midland Red buses got priority over other traffic! Five bob is 25p in today's money but was not to be sneezed at in the inter-war years. Attwoods was a wonderful department store spreading through all these buildings with small rooms and corridors connecting them. It was later demolished and replaced by a typical 1960s store. *Midland Red*

Opposite: This looks like a trial shot for the famous Beatles album cover, with a fab FEDD instead of the Fab Four. 1938 Brush-bodied 2135, with only the lower deck rebuilt, is outbound on London Road, Leicester, in October 1957 with a Corporation all-Leyland PD2 behind. The pedestrian crossing leads to the railway station off-camera on the right. *F W York/ Transport Museum Wythall*

Three of the first Brush-bodied batch were built with full width cabs. Presumably encouraged by the SLRs, this was a belated attempt to join the 1930s streamlining movement although it has to be said the overall FEDD design was not a promising candidate. It could hardly be described as sleek and, worse, SOS front ends were asymmetric with radiators slightly offset to the nearside. The poor access to the engine on these three must have been annoying so they were converted to half-cab as early as 1940. EHA 290 was later numbered 2158. It is seen here at Dudley on 1 August 1938. Later part of the West Midlands county, Dudley at this time was an island of Worcestershire entirely surrounded by Staffordshire. *R T Coxon/ Transport Museum Wythall*

Another 1938 EHA FEDD that received an experimental front end was 2167 (EHA 299) but, this time, the result was highly significant. This full-width bonnet and concealed radiator were fitted in 1942, the concept being registered by the company on 2 January 1943. Midland Red thus set the pace with concealed radiators and would fit them to all its post-war standard vehicles. 2167, however, reverted to exposed radiator upon its body rebuild in 1951. It is seen here at Walsall's bus station on St Paul's Street with a more typical example of 1943 bus design behind, an 'austerity' Weymann-bodied Daimler CWA6 allocated to the company by the Ministry of War Transport. *R A Mills/ Transport Museum Wythall*

Stourbridge Town railway station opened in 1879 as the original station was too far from the town centre. The track between Stourbridge Town and Junction stations is thought to be the shortest operational branch line in Europe. The Town building was demolished a century later, being replaced by much reduced facilities. Until then, Town station provided an impressive backdrop to the buses loading there such as FEDD 2219 working local route S50 to High Park estate on 17 September 1957. *Peter Mitchell*

The FEDDs were cosy, smooth-running buses that performed well into their old age but the stencil route numbers were not clear unless lit from behind. The spare number stencils would rattle in their holder inside the destination box - 2232 is on the K10, which ran to Lickhill, a suburb of Stourport off the Bewdley Road, seen here. The destination blind has been left at Kidderminster while the route board on the bulkhead gives the current destination. Conductors had to collect all the boards for their duty before leaving the garage – there could be several of them as a number of 'locals' might be worked in the same duty. The Old Judge Tea adverts were a regular feature of the FEDDs. There is little traffic on 17 September 1957 but 2232 is followed by a 'Bradford' van, built by Jowett between 1947 and 1953. *Peter Mitchell*

Many Midland Red services made their way along Broad Street, Birmingham, seen here in July 1959. They would continue along Hagley Road where the company's buses outnumbered those of Birmingham City Transport. Some services turned off along Sandon Road to reach Langley and beyond, including the 123 to Causeway Green, worked here by FEDD 2231, being pursued by an LD8 Leyland. *F W York/ Transport Museum Wythall*

The long 144 route from Birmingham to the Malverns was very successful and double-deck buses were reintroduced in the mid-1930s. The weekday frequency became every 20 minutes, increased to a 15-minute headway on Saturdays with massive duplication on bank holidays. FEDD 2236 is seen in Bromsgrove on 4 July 1953, outside the Coach & Horses at the junction of High Street and Alcester Road. There was another Alcester Road not far to the north through Lickey End and Burcot so this one was renamed Stratford Road around 1970. The Coach & Horses has since been demolished, see page 115. 2236 was evidently one of the FEDDs that only needed rebuilding of its lower deck. *Peter Mitchell*

Redditch-allocated FEDD 2244 passes Studley's police station on Alcester Road, in July 1957. A new police station replaced this which has since been demolished but you can still admire the older building, even if you can't find a police officer. *F W York/ Transport Museum Wythall*

Production of FEDDs and SONs continued until 1940 when war intervened. The last 50 of both classes had more rounded bodies, particularly the rear dome. 2370 is seen at the island in the centre of Blackheath during August 1957. *F W York/ Transport Museum Wythall*

Only a short step from Pritchards with your macs and Daks slacks onto the H8 local bus service loading outside in High Town, Hereford. Unusual to see 2336 in the city as FEDDs were not allocated there until the 1950s by which time they were quite old. *Lyndon W Row*

This is Station Street, Birmingham, which was first used as a terminus by Midland Red buses in 1922. Further services were soon transferred there and a large, long shelter was erected. On fine bank holidays, Midland Red inspectors in Station Street and the Bull Ring would face half the population of Birmingham seeking rides to attractive destinations throughout the Midlands. A Birmingham City Transport inspector would be dealing with the other half in Navigation Street, loading trams to the Lickeys. Crews were placed on standby whenever the weather offered the likelihood of crowds. One of the most popular attractions in the Tamworth area is Drayton Manor Park, once home of former Prime Minister Sir Robert Peel. Like many grand estates, costs meant the old manor house was eventually demolished and the grounds languished. Shortly after World War Two, a pleasure park and zoo was established that quickly went from strength to strength. The attraction was principally served by the 198 Birmingham-Tamworth service, normally hourly and almost entirely worked by Tamworth garage. Here are FEDD 2336 and D7 4407, both evidently providing bank holiday reliefs in 1958. Station Street was much shortened at this end by the construction of the Bull Ring Shopping Centre, including Midland Red's fully undercover bus station opened on 1 November 1963. The new Bull Ring Bus Station brought all the company's Birmingham services into one central terminus for the first time (except the Dudley Road group jointly operated with Birmingham City Transport out of Edmund Street and long-distance services which continued to use Digbeth Coach Station). *F W York/ Transport Museum Wythall*

Kidderminster is famous for carpet manufacture and the good years brought some impressive buildings. In the background is the headquarters of Brinton's carpets, in front of its town centre factory. To the left is the College of Further Education; the right-half of a building shared with the Public Library just out of shot. To the right is the Post Office, outside which FEDD 2360 has just left the K26 stand in Exchange Street and is turning into Market Street on 17 September 1957. The driver on the platform is probably hitching a lift to the staff canteen at the other end of Market Street! 2360 will shortly climb Comberton Hill past the railway station, today famous for its heritage trains. Small boys are nabbing the long front seat upstairs, and one has noticed the photographer! Nab is an appropriate word for this area around this time as the local Member of Parliament was the colourful Sir Gerald Nabarro whose cars carried Worcestershire registrations NAB 1 upwards. *Peter Mitchell*

Opposite top: FEDD 2351 on 13 September 1957 works the S88 local service along Newport Road, Stafford, with a wartime Guy double-decker of independent operator Austin's of Woodseaves in the background. *Peter Mitchell*

Opposite: Bromsgrove has grown considerably in recent years and the railway facilities have only recently received major investment, including electrification. Back in May 1957, FEDD 2342 is still to decide whether it is a B23 or 323 from Bromsgrove Station to Sidemoor. Its old school driver distrusts the handbrake and has rolled the bus back into the kerb. *F W York/ Transport Museum Wythall*

Birmingham's Dudley Road group of services were an exception to the 1914 agreement between Midland Red and Birmingham City Transport. Midland Red's Oldbury garage opened on 12 April 1937 but its main work did not begin until 1 October 1939 when Midland Red buses, operating on behalf of the local authorities along the route to the west of the Birmingham boundary, replaced the BCT trams working the Birmingham – Smethwick – Oldbury - Dudley route. Oldbury received around 35 new FEDDs, one of the largest single allocations by the company of one batch of buses. The tram connection meant the route was nicknamed 'The Track' (not the only 'Track' on the company's network!) The Dudley Road group included short workings and spurs to Bearwood and Soho, the whole group being numbered B80 to B89, theoretically jointly worked by Midland Red and BCT. In practice, each service was largely run by either Midland Red or BCT, the B for Birmingham prefixes being carried by BCT buses too. Unlike the rest of the city, this meant Midland Red shared the all-stops local service function inside Birmingham. FHA-registered FEDDs remained familiar on the Dudley Road for very many years. 2372 is seen at Steward Street, inbound to Birmingham. Following in the distance is a Birmingham City Transport Leyland PD2/Park Royal; BCT drivers were very good at 'pushing' a bus in front, especially if from another garage or, even better in this case, another operator! *F W York/ Transport Museum Wythall*

Buses linger on the wide piece of land in front of Digbeth garage shortly before it was reclaimed by Birmingham Corporation. They are standing on what became the dual carriageway of Digbeth in the mid-1950s. The garage and coach station was to the left of the photographer and itself would be reconstructed in 1958. On the left is D5B 3810 but the three FEDDs are an interesting collection. The body of 2341 was rebuilt by Nudd instead of the usual contractor at Hooton. 2161 has only had its lower deck rebuilt while 1819, like all the Metro-Cammell-bodied FEDDs, has not needed any significant attention. The opening of Sheepcote Street garage in August 1951 and the takeover of part of the Walsall Road group of bus services by Birmingham City Transport in 1957-8 took much of the steam out of Digbeth's overcrowding problem. *Ken Swallow*

'Hey lads, this isn't fair!' This busy scene at Walsall Bus Station shows the Nudd-rebuilt FEDD 2341 on the 118 with three then modern D7s on its tail in March 1957. The FEDDs were light and, if well maintained, could keep up with D7s and LD8s while AD2s and D5s could not. The busy industrial town of Walsall had its own municipal transport department and, contrary to the impression given by this picture, Midland Red was very much the minor operator. The road between Birmingham and Walsall, however, used to be a major activity for Midland Red. Services commenced on Christmas Eve 1913 and received the 118 identification in the 1928 renumbering. Short workings followed, mainly at the Birmingham end including a branch to Beeches Estate. Eventually so many buses were required that four garages were involved, Bearwood, Digbeth, Sutton Coldfield and Sheepcote Street. Most of the short workings became entirely within Birmingham following extension of the city boundary in 1928. By agreement the services continued to be run by the company until, in 1957-8, Birmingham City Transport took over the Beeches Estate journeys, and short workings between the city centre and the Scott Arms, leaving the company with just the core 118 to Walsall. Midland Red presence was further reduced from 8 August 1968 when the 118 became jointly operated with Walsall Corporation. West Midlands PTE took over Birmingham and Walsall's municipal buses in 1969 and mopped up Midland Red's share of the 118 on 3 December 1973. *F W York/ Transport Museum Wythall*

While Midland Red's D5B, D7 and LD8 buses might have been warmer than the open platform Birmingham City Transport buses that replaced them on the Walsall Road, one of the ways the company had made itself unpopular was to provide single-deckers when two decks were required. Here is 1940 SON 2430 at the Scott Arms but this single-deck cloud has a silver lining as it allows us to see the sign for a Midland Red booking agency above the bus. The agency is a perhaps surprising offshoot of Mr Lowe's grocery and provisions business. 2430 and the BHA FEDD behind are on short workings. Some early post-war Carlyle body rebuilds were not very obvious and are probably better described as heavy overhauls. 2430 remained largely in original condition, the limited reconditioning of its Brush body being indicated by the metal strip over the windows replacing the original glass louvres. Buses receiving such limited attention had shortened lives, 2430 being withdrawn as early as 1952. *Malcolm Keeley collection*

2384 demonstrates the well-rounded rear of the last 50 SONs. This is Corporation Street, Birmingham, and 2384 is overtaking a 1948 Metro-Cammell bodied Daimler CVG6 of the city's transport department. C & A Modes was a familiar fashion store on Corporation Street and is filling the gap caused by wartime bombing as creatively as possible. *Transport Museum Wythall collection*

The local authority constructed the bus station off Commercial Road, Hereford, in 1934 on the site of a former prison. The prison governor originally occupied the building seen behind SON 2398 with rebuilt body on 26 June 1954. The premises contained, in its new form, passenger enquiry offices for both Midland Red and Red & White until the 1970s. It also included Midland Red's Traffic Offices as the garage was over a mile away, the latter being an engineering establishment only. *Ken Swallow*

World War Two caused bus production throughout the UK to be halted in 1940. A number of buses were finished off and distributed to operators by the Ministry of War Transport in 1942, Midland Red receiving nine Leyland and six AEC double-deckers. Three of the Leylands carried bodies by Northern Counties to the very rounded style it favoured in the late 1930s. 2438 is seen on Railway Drive, Wolverhampton, loading for Stourbridge. *R T Wilson/ Transport Museum Wythall*

Sheer need caused bus production to resume nationally in 1942, although on a much reduced scale. Midland Red, for example, carried 210 million passengers in 1939 but this had risen to nearly 330 million in 1944. Bus bodies, irrespective of manufacturer, would be built to a severe specification set by the Ministry of Supply to simplify production and reduce the materials needed, including unradiused rear domes. The new buses had either Guy Arab or Daimler chassis, Midland Red receiving a quantity of both, almost entirely with bodies to the MoS austerity specification. Guys and Daimlers looking like this were delivered to operators all over the UK. Daimler CWA6 2547 with Brush 56-seat body was one of many wartime buses to be delivered with wooden slatted seats although Midland Red ensured they received upholstered seats as soon as possible after the war. It is seen loading at Walsall bus station. *R A Mills/ Transport Museum Wythall*

Here is Daimler 2547 again, after body rebuilding by Willowbrook, at the Bull Ring terminus, Birmingham, in the company of S12 3737. Most of the wartime bus bodies deteriorated quickly due to the necessity of using unseasoned timber for the frames. They were rebuilt fairly early in life and, as well as going to the trouble of fitting post-war destination boxes, Midland Red took the opportunity to soften their appearance in a number of ways. Rounded rear domes and radiused glazing were improvements made by many operators but Midland Red went one step further by building up the front wings, rendering them stylistically in a world of their own! All this effort by the company to extend the lives of pre-war and wartime buses may seem strange when nearly 1,000 new post-war buses were in service by the end of 1952. Annual passenger numbers, however, had risen to 462 million by that time, reducing the number of older buses that could be replaced. In the case of the wartime buses, the refurbishment may only have partially delayed the deterioration as Midland Red sold off these non-standard buses at around eleven years of age, although most found new owners. *Transport Museum Wythall*

The Guy rebuilds were, in almost all cases, handled by Brush using a different style of sliding ventilators. 2506 is seen on 9 April 1955 at St Margarets bus station, Leicester, in the company of Kemp & Shaw Leyland GRY 763. Kemp & Shaw was taken over by Midland Red on 31 July 1955 but operated as a subsidiary until full absorption on 1 January 1959, at which time GRY 763 became bus 4844 with its new owner. Despite being the only 'low bridge' (side gangway upstairs) bus in the Midland Red fleet, the 1950 vehicle ran until 1967. *Peter Mitchell*

The six 1942 AECs mentioned earlier had Brush bodies to a style that originally clearly revealed them to be part of a Coventry Corporation order, perhaps surprisingly not delivered to that devastated city. Even these received the front end alterations plus flush mounted windows with sliding vents as demonstrated here by 2444 at Wednesbury. Retaining and rebuilding these six non-standard buses may seem a bit strange but, under the bonnet, they were very similar to the 100 early post-war AD2s. AEC diesel engines also powered the DON single-deckers, the wartime Daimlers and 40 of the 135 Metro-Cammell bodied FEDDs of 1935-6 converted from petrol to diesel (the rest received BMMO 'K' engines). *R A Mills/ Transport Museum Wythall*

The eastern end of Birmingham's New Street continued to be an important commencing point for Midland Red services to the north and east of the city. Photographed in much the same location as BHA 361 (page 34), you can see the changes over twenty years caused by wartime bombing and redevelopment since the mid-1930s with a large blitzed site standing empty behind the Guy. Midland Red's wartime Guys were shared between Sutton Coldfield and Leicester's Sandacre Street garages; 2557 (HHA 9) belonged to the former. The D5B alongside is 3788 emphasising the transition after the war to rear-entrance double-deckers following experience with the wartime utility buses. A wartime Daimler stands behind. *Midland Red*

Midland Reds from New Street turned right into Corporation Street where a rebuilt utility Daimler is being followed by several Birmingham City Transport buses. Lewis's wonderful department store occupied the corner of Corporation Street and Bull Street and you were allowed access to the roof. Children, for a small charge, could enjoy Austin pedal cars up there when they weren't hanging over the parapet trying to read the numbers of buses several storeys below. The roof also provided a handy site for the photographer. Many of the nearer buildings have been replaced in this part of Corporation Street and normal traffic is no longer allowed, today only a Midland Metro tramcar is available to flatten inattentive pedestrians. Lewis's store sadly has closed but its buildings and thus the photographer's standpoint remain. *Midland Red*

Birmingham's one-way system then required the Midland Reds to turn left from Corporation Street into Bull Street; Midland Metro follows the same route today. Buses of the two operators make the manoeuvre, the leading Midland Red is another wartime Daimler. The buildings seen here have all been replaced. The new arrangements included a replacement arcade, soulless in comparison, for the original seen beside the Daimler. *Midland Red*

Wartime Daimler 2540 has arrived at the loading stops in New Street. It is interesting to see, next to the Odeon cinema, C & A Modes (Coats & 'Ats) occupying some of the retail space below King Edward House until rebuilding of its Corporation Street store (see page 50) after war damage was finally achieved. The conductor passes a message to the driver of 2540 from the inspector. The Willowbrook refurbishments did not quite submerge distinctive features of the original bodybuilders; 2540 retains the raised lower edge of the cab windows employed by Duple. *Lyndon W Rowe*

The ease of leaving buses lounging around Birmingham city centre in the early post-war years will leave today's motorists honking with laughter. The photographer finding this bus in Jamaica Row immediately identified it as different. Midland Red built four experimental rear-engine single-deckers in the mid-1930s. These were rebuilt to underfloor engines during World War Two as prototypes for post-war production and given type designations S1 to S4. An all-new prototype, the S5, followed in 1946 which additionally pioneered chassisless construction, a development later adopted on the S14 onwards. This is S3 no 1943, familiarly known as Charlie Two because of its registration. It is another duplicate pressed into use on the 198, serving Drayton Manor Park, this time during the factory holiday period on 24 July 1954. The 1943 rebuild of the body moved several steps closer to the styling of the first production underfloor engine buses, the S6 class, although it should be noted its post-war destination box was a later modification. *Ken Swallow*

The post-war buses began a new fleet number series from 3000 upwards. On May Day 1947 around ten new S6s were driven through central Birmingham and aroused considerable interest, including local press coverage, the parade being seen here in Corporation Street with 3070 prominent. The May 1947 edition of the Staff Information Bulletin reported that 61 of the S6 underfloor-engine buses were now in service, operating from 17 garages. It was intended that every garage would have at least one S6 when all 100 (3000-3099) had been delivered. The S6s were revolutionary in appearance; at this time Birmingham City Transport still had to rely entirely on pre-war and wartime vehicles. *Midland Red/ The Bus Archive*

S6 3011, into service at the dawn of 1947, is seen around a mile east of Bridgnorth heading towards Enville. It will continue on through Kinver and Stourbridge from where it will follow the frequent 130 route into Birmingham. One of Foxall's Bedfords has come from the RAF camp at Stanmore and will turn right to terminate in Bridgnorth where the operator was based. Foxall's bus service was originally intended for RAF personnel, their families and other workers at the camp. Foxall preferred coach specification vehicles, usually Bedfords, as excursions and private hire provided most of its business which was sold to Whittle of Highley in 1976. As 1960 moved into 1961, Midland Red's Scottish general manager Donald Sinclair could celebrate Hogmanay in the knowledge that the last pre-war vehicles had come out of service and, from now on, his latest products would be replacing the early post-war fleet like 3011. These were the first generation of buses designed under his management but he did not seem to hold any sentimental affection for them.
Transport Museum Wythall

Prior to the opening of Banbury's bus station, buses used to cluster in the area of the Town Hall. The maximum width for buses for many years was 7 feet 6 inches. This was relaxed to 8 feet shortly after World War Two and Midland Red started construction of wider service buses as soon as possible. The first BMMO buses to the new width were S8s 3200-99 and S9s 3357-3456, almost all in service by the end of 1949 when single-deck buses in the rest of the country were still largely being built with front engines. S9 3418 with S6 3095 at Banbury flank a City of Oxford 1944 Guy Arab II with Roe austerity bodywork, JWL 910. Keen aficionados will spot that the front styling on the wider buses was subtly changed from the S6. Initially operators had to apply for special authorisation on each route to be worked by the eight-footers. The extra six inches was divided equally, two inches on each of the two double passenger seats and the remaining two in the gangway, making life more comfortable for the conductor as well as the passengers. *Transport Museum Wythall*

Upton-on-Severn used to be a small inland port handling goods brought upriver from Bristol and Gloucester. It has buildings of several periods, notably Tudor timber-framed cottages and bow-windowed Georgian houses. It is not immune from changes, however, as the two buildings directly behind S6 3036 in New Street have been redeveloped. By the time of this photograph around 1959, the 362 comprised two round journeys on Wednesdays and Saturdays from Worcester to Upton. The Saturday journeys were extended via Longdon Heath and Castlemorton to Rye Cross. All the early post-war single-decker service buses were lengthened from 27 feet 6 inches to 29 feet 3 inches between 1951 and 1953 following a relaxation to 30 feet in permitted dimensions from 1 June 1950. This allowed an extra row of seats, increasing capacity from 40 to 44. Fortunately the back axles were relatively far back so the rear overhang did not become excessive as 3036 demonstrates. It was withdrawn in September 1961 but was unusual in enjoying a second life. It was sold to a building contractor based in Kidderminster which used it as mobile accommodation on building contracts in remote areas of Scotland. Most fortunately it was rescued from Perth for a third life in preservation at the Transport Museum Wythall. *Ken Jubb*

Passengers board 1948 S8 3264 in Rugeley, alongside the old Market Hall. *Transport Museum Wythall*

The 499 ran between Banbury and Charlton where S9 3374 awaits its return journey on 16 April 1960. A few journeys were extended to the delightfully-named and deeply rural Hinton-in-the-Hedges on Banbury's market days, Thursdays and Saturdays, but these were withdrawn by the end of the 1960s. *Peter Mitchell*

A fascinating scene of Midland Red buses loading in The Square, Shrewsbury, with its statue of Robert Clive (Clive of India), the town's MP from 1761 to 1774. Timekeeping hopefully is improved by the clock on the old market hall. The picture was taken shortly before the new bus station off Barker Street opened. While much of the stock on view may imply an earlier date, contrasting on the left with the antiques is S9 3368, allocated to Shrewsbury from new in 1949. *Michael H C Baker collection*

Opposite top: Among the 100 S9 buses was an important prototype. General Manager Donald Sinclair visited the USA in late 1948 to investigate transport arrangements in the USA and Canada, gathering ideas on bus design and operation. 3441 did not appear until 1950 and the frontal design with powered entrance doors, recessed windscreens and heavy brow does reflect American single-deckers of the period. Midland Red could not resist plenty of brightwork, perhaps another sign of American brashness, 3441 hinting at more luxury than it actually provided as it was to bus standard. 3441 is beginning another portion of work at Leicester, pulling into Gravel Street from Sandacre Street garage with its clock above the company's enquiry office. This garage was very conveniently located with St Margaret's Bus Station to the left of the photographer. It ceased to be a bus garage years ago but the building still exists. *Transport Museum Wythall*

Opposite: A service between Northampton and Birmingham was introduced as the 196 on 8 December 1928, being renumbered X96 on 25 February 1929. The famous X96 was extended from 12 April 1930 westwards to Shrewsbury to become one of the longest stage carriage routes in the country with around 150 fare stages over the 101 miles. In this form it ran every four hours and became much beloved by Midland Red aficionados with Day Anywhere tickets, although few would have made the end-to-end journey of over five hours. The X96 became a true limited stop service from 2 September 1967 and was joined by the X93/4/5, effectively 'short' workings of the principal service jointly providing an hourly frequency between Birmingham and Wolverhampton. The introduction of the motorway system eventually greatly improved point-to-point timings but, in time, the famous route gradually shrank to nothing. S8s 3217/37/41 were rebuilt with S15 fronts and improved seating in 1957-8, initially being frequently used on the X96 in their refurbished form. S8 3237 is loading in Fisher Street, Dudley, one of the level bus stops in this hilly town centre. *Ken Jubb*

The opening of Shrewsbury's Barker Street bus station gave relief to the crowded town centre with its treasure of Tudor and Elizabethan buildings. The new bus station had its own architectural delights, not least its backdrop of Rowley's House, a sprawling 16th century former Tudor merchant's home, now a museum. Barker Street bus station closed in 1989. Midland Red had exclusive use of this bus station which included a company enquiry office. The double-decker prominent in the centre is D5B 3859, the other is an AD2. S9s 3377 and 3378 are also visible. The SON with a sliding door just leaving the bus station is 1883 (CHA 507). To the side of the D5B is CON 1520 (HA 9471). Use of double-deck buses at Shrewsbury was hampered by the low bridge next to the railway station. *Geoff Charles collection by permission of Llyfrgell Genedlaethol Cymru/The National Library of Wales.*

The large forecourt of Stourbridge garage on the corner of Foster Street and St John's Road became the town's bus station with a Booking and Enquiry Office. Increasing demand meant that a second bus station was opened across the road on the forecourt of Stourbridge Town Station. This delightful picture shows a fine selection of cars trying to exit St John's Road and S9 3387 in front of the garage decorated for the 1953 Coronation of Queen Elizabeth II. The garage was reconstructed in 1958, extending over the forecourt so that the buses loading there were now under cover and available for overnight bus parking. Unfortunately this introduced the mixed use problems of fumes and dirt that, on a much larger scale, would beset Birmingham's Bull Ring bus station, opened a few years later. *Midland Red/ The Bus Archive*

After World War Two, many services were converted to double-deck buses to provide much needed extra capacity. The double-decking of the busy 130 Birmingham-Stourbridge service became possible from 8 May 1948 when a third bus station was opened in Stourbridge off Vauxhall Road, on the Birmingham side of the Foster Street railway bridge. The latter has long been swept away but in those days it was impossible for double-deckers from Birmingham to reach the town's primary bus station without a long detour. Midland Red's own BMMO production immediately after World War Two at first concentrated on underfloor-engine single-deckers as all the outside manufacturers were still offering only vertical engine models. So, when requirements exceeded BMMO's abilities, it was double-deckers that were ordered from outside manufacturers. The AD2s were the first double-deck order, no less than 100 AEC Regent II buses numbered 3100-99, to receive bodies to Midland Red design based on the D1 late wartime prototype. The first 12 post-war double-deckers converted the 130 service; 3100-1 allocated to Bearwood, 3102-3 to Cradley Heath and 3104-11 to Stourbridge's own garage. Passengers alight from 3111 in the new bus station, the troublesome railway line over Foster Street is on the extreme left. *Transport Museum Wythall*

British Railways took over the existing railway companies on 1 January 1948 and its Wolverhampton assets included two central stations. This is another view of Railway Drive, but from a different angle. The ex-LNWR High Level station structures seen here would be completely replaced between 1964 and 1967 during electrification. The ex-GWR Low Level station lost its trains but ironically its buildings survived, initially as a Parcels Concentration Depot. 3147 was another AD2 at Stourbridge garage, spending nearly all its life there, surviving until May 1962. *The Omnibus Society/ The Bus Archive*

The first operations at Hereford commenced in March 1920 using just three primitive Tilling-Stevens buses on several routes to nearby towns and villages; a breakdown would leave some routes without a service until the bus was repaired. These buses operated from the yard of the Black Lion hotel, but in 1925 a purpose-built garage was opened and by the 1940s there was an allocation of 45-50 vehicles. The garage was somewhat basic compared to others built by the company around this time but the structure proved extremely long-lived and survived until recently. The AD2s were not very nimble with relatively small engines and fairly heavy bodies, so most were gradually gathered at garages with less challenging terrain. 3149 works a Hereford local service from the Shire Hall with its fine Doric columns and was one of 50 bodied by Brush delivered in 1948. The remaining 50 bodies were handled by Metro-Cammell, nearly all being delayed until 1950 - by which time Midland Red had not only constructed the first 100 of its own D5 double-deck chassis but had received them from coachbuilder Brush. *Lyndon W Rowe*

The driver of D5 3496 tackles the island at the Holly Bush on Hagley Road West, Quinton, Birmingham. The 100 BMMO D5s were built to the new width of 8 feet and numbered 3457-3556. D5 3496, new in 1949, was garaged at Hartshill as the company liked to spell it, much to the frustration of the late photographer (a Midland Red employee) who always correctly insisted the garage was in Harts Hill! *S E Letts*

Midland Red buses were brought into the Dudley area during 1924 to deal with opposition buses competing over the BET-owned tramway routes and then they replaced the trams themselves. The addition of other routes meant a dense Midland Red network rapidly developed. The municipal operators ran a few services into Dudley, including Wolverhampton's trolleybuses, but Midland Red basically ruled the roost. Midland Red's Dudley garage opened on 2 August 1929 and was among those passed to the West Midlands PTE in December 1973. The takeover arguably had the greatest impact in Dudley; only the X96 family of long-distance services survived and even they were soon re-routed, ending Midland Red's huge association with the town. Many of the local services, for which D prefix letters were introduced on 1 October 1934, were very challenging in terms of gradient and road surfaces. The power-to-weight ratio of the 1949 GD6 class Guys, 3557-3576, was very welcome on Dudley's hills and they almost entirely worked from that town's garage – even after the original big Meadows engines were replaced by BMMO 8 litre units. This is Cradley Heath station on 23 September 1958. *Peter Mitchell*

The 245/6 (Stourbridge-Dudley-Wednesbury) in early post-war years required around 25 buses, largely supplied by Hartshill (or Harts Hill!) but Dudley and Stourbridge also contributed. 3576 is at Harts Hill on 17 September 1957 and, being one of the 1949 GD6s, must be on a working from Dudley garage. The local cinema may be showing the classic film 'Hell Drivers' starring Stanley Baker and every other British male actor of note, driving at breakneck speed a fleet of surprisingly energetic 'parrot-nose' Dodge tipper lorries like these. The drivers here have time to enjoy the Pantry Café but, unlike the film, the comely Jill Ireland may not be serving the tea. *Peter Mitchell*

Midland Red's photographer carried out a wide range of duties, including recording accident scenes and difficult road layouts. On 28 October 1960 he went to Oakeywell Street with GD6 3576 to photograph the extreme camber of the road. While well within the 28-degree tilt angle required of double-decker buses, it would be very uncomfortable for everyone on board and at risk from roadside lighting columns. Roads around Dudley also suffered subsidence from abandoned coal mine tunnels. *Midland Red/ The Bus Archive*

A splendid view of traffic in Paradise Street, Birmingham. Many of the buildings have since gone but all is not lost as the best, notably the Town Hall, remain. In the background the buildings on 'Galloway's Corner' have been replaced by an enlargement of Victoria Square. Midland Metro now runs along Paradise Street. Back in the 1950s, a classic wartime Bedford truck, produced in this case with civilian cab and military front end, looks for a trailer to haul while the Midland Red contributions are a D5B on the 122 to Oldbury via Langley and a GD6 to Dudley via Blackheath. Birmingham City Transport buses, mostly Daimlers, are everywhere. *Midland Red*

Midland Red's coaches faced a different kind of lane – parking lanes - at Birmingham's Digbeth Coach Station, seen here after completion of remodelling in 1958. This is a quiet scene showing C1 3334 alongside a Royal Blue Bristol MW but Digbeth could be very busy indeed at times. August Bank Holiday used to be at the beginning of the month, coinciding with the end of the Birmingham factory holiday. The following rounded statistics were reported over three days of the Bank Holiday weekend in 1952:

Friday 1 August.   5,000 holidaymakers outward; 6,000 returning
Saturday 2 August.   9,000 holidaymakers outward; 10,000 returning
Sunday 3 August.   6,000 holidaymakers outward; 7,000 returning

Just after World War Two only the 50 SLR and 25 ONC vehicles survived in the coach fleet, earlier coaches having been disposed of or converted to buses. Fortunately the SLRs and ONCs were modern looking, there were not any half-cab coaches in the fleet. Nevertheless the arrival of the C1 (3300-3344) express coaches and C2 (3345-3356) touring coaches in 1948-50 was very welcome. Approval had to be gained on each route proposed for 8 feet wide vehicles so, because they were required to go almost anywhere, the C1 and C2 coaches were built to the earlier width of 7 feet 6 inches. Midland Red's coaches had a comparatively easy life in the pre-motorway era, over half being stored over the winter months. This gave them the opportunity of long lives although, of course, elderly coaches were frowned upon by discerning travellers. The modern looking and highly polished C1s and C2s aged well and Midland Red got away with using most of them until 1965. *Midland Red/ The Bus Archive*

Adolf Hitler apparently took a fancy to Bridgnorth and considered it a possible place for relaxation after successfully invading the UK. The Severn has carved out a deep valley and a funicular links the resultant Low and High Towns. North Gate in the High Town is the last of Bridgnorth's five medieval gateways to survive and dates back to around 1250. S10 3588 is entering High Street while working the B90 town service in August 1961. The Burlingham-bodied coach belongs to Whittle's of Highley, at this time replacing most of its fleet annually, enhancing the independent's reputation hugely. *Transport Museum Wythall*

Opposite: A nostalgic view of local shops in Hinckley Road, Leicester, near Coventry Street, with the bus approaching the Narborough Road junction. Although service 725 between Nuneaton and Leicester was established first, the 658 from Coventry and Hinckley via Nuneaton became the principal service to and from Leicester. 725s basically became Monday to Friday peak and Saturday extras, other short workings were the 726 and 727. Double-deck operation became possible after the road was lowered under a bridge in Hinckley Road, Nuneaton. Construction of a further 200 single-deckers began with bus 3577 in 1949. They were mostly of a slightly modified design styled the S10 but later examples 3733-76 took advantage of the new length of 30 feet permitted from 1 June 1950 and were designated S12. Hinckley-allocated S10 3683 is obviously in its earliest days, being still 27 feet 6 inches long, but, like all the early post-war single-deckers, it would soon be extended to the new length. *Transport Museum Wythall*

Financial difficulties caused Corvedale of Ludlow to sell some of its routes to Midland Red in May 1953. S10 3661 has just arrived from Bridgnorth on an ex-Corvedale service and awaits its next move alongside Ludlow's Town Hall. Corvedale continued with its other services until the proprietor retired in 1965 and sold the business to Yeomans of Canon Pyon which passed it on to Whittle of Highley in 1969. Both Yeomans and Whittle retained Corvedale's separate identity until the latter fully absorbed it in 1981. *Lyndon W Rowe*

This busy scene at Hereford's bus station shows the fine turnout of the Midland Red buses based in the city. S10 3624 is the leading vehicle with two S6s behind, including 3035. *Lyndon W Rowe*

Close to Worcester's Shrub Hill railway station on Shrub Hill Road was a pair of semaphore signals for those road users that could understand them. Those that didn't could have a close encounter with a train on a single-track works branch line that notably served Worcester Vinegar Works, hence it was known as the Vinegar branch! S10 3626 crosses the track on 8 August 1964. As noted earlier, the 355 was an infrequent service which did not run to the same timetable on any two consecutive days. *Lyndon W Rowe*

Swadlincote-based S10 3653 and S12 3751 are seen working services in the pleasant country town of Ashby-de-la-Zouch around 1960. The full 697 service between Ashby-de-la-Zouch and Nuneaton, jointly operated by Swadlincote and Nuneaton garages, had replaced LMS trains as far back as 1931 but was itself withdrawn after 31 August 1971. The 722 Ashby – Measham service was taken over in 1937 from C W Moore. The Ashby - Appleby Magna journeys on the latter were renumbered 697 from November 1953 but reverted to 722 when the full route was withdrawn. The 722 was replaced when the 677 Coalville - Heather service was extended to Appleby Magna, Measham and Ashby from 31 May 1980. *Transport Museum Wythall*

Opposite top: Both Midland Red and Barton Transport commenced Birmingham – Nottingham services in September 1928. Between Birmingham and Tamworth, Midland Red ran its X99 via Sutton Coldfield while Barton went via Tyburn House, Curdworth and Fazeley. The competition was ended by a service swap, effective from 22 February 1932. Barton took over BMMO's Leicester-Nottingham operation and, in exchange, BMMO took on the Barton service as its X98, running this variant until 23 September 1939 when cuts were applied after the outbreak of World War Two. Standard saloons were usually employed on the X99 before the arrival of dual-purpose types like the S13 and S15, and duplicates were frequently required. The S12s were the first production buses to take advantage of the longer permitted dimension of 30 feet and the extra four seats would have been useful. 3763 is seen when new at the Parade, Sutton Coldfield – this particular bus ran for some years with a Leyland O600 engine which must have been worth listening to! Sutton Coldfield, with its magnificent park, was added to Birmingham as recently as 1974. *Gordon Davies*

Opposite: S12 3755 spent most of its life at Kidderminster and is seen returning to the town centre along George Street, approaching the junction with Station Hill. The conductor has already reset the blinds for its next trip on the K17 which did not run along here. Laughton Goodwin shows a range of Austin cars of the early 1950s, while in the foreground is a Jowett 'Bradford' van. Behind the bus is the former garage of P Owen and Sons of Abberley, whose business was acquired by Midland Red in November 1938. Part of it was used by the Ministry of Aircraft Production in the Second World War for theproduction of small parts, but it was only briefly employed operationally by Midland Red due to the poor access and was eventually sold in 1957. *Roger Torode collection*

S12 3754 on Hereford local service H3 to Green Lanes loads outside St Peter's Church, just one of the city's many fine ecclesiastical buildings, on 27 August 1962. *Ken Swallow*

The market town of Evesham, enjoying the River Avon and at the heart of the fertile Vale that bears its name, is still most attractive today but, in the years before foreign holiday breaks, took on the feel of an inland resort during the summer months. Midland Red would bring in the crowds while other buses quietly got on with the everyday business of serving the local population. This is S10 3676 in Peewit Road, Hampton, on 3 August 1963; the conductor has jammed himself on the platform while passengers board and alight. *Peter Mitchell*

This is a familiar spot to anybody who has travelled on a bus from the Transport Museum, Wythall, showing the Horse & Jockey in that village in July 1958 when the main A435 literally passed the door. The shallow valley was carved out by the infant River Cole, just beginning its long run around the east of Birmingham before draining into the River Tame. This is now one of the slip roads leading up to the A435 dual carriageway carried on an overpass over the valley and 3784 of Evesham garage is travelling in the wrong direction of today's traffic. A further 100 Brush-bodied D5 double-deckers were built in 1950-2, numbered 3777-3876. Following successful trials using the D1 post-war prototype double-decker, this second batch had power-operated platform doors and was known as the D5B class. The doors made them ideal for services such as the 148 which took nearly two hours to travel between Evesham and Birmingham, operating on an hourly frequency, duplicated as required on weekends and bank holidays. *F W York/ Transport Museum Wythall*

Miss Marple has checked out the Lenches, the Littletons and the Combertons. Murder suspects? No, groups of villages in the Evesham area. Her current mystery is how to get back to St Mary Mead – sorry, luv, not on the Midland Red network. Try the Stratford Blue and Bristol Tramways timetable cases or perhaps Midland Red's enquiry office in the town will be able to help. Shiny D5B 3790 has Birmingham Digbeth blinds and thus cannot provide a proper display for local service 394 to Offenham. If this is a holiday extra dispatched from Birmingham on the 148 and then collared by the Evesham inspector, the Brummie crew eyeing the photographer may have their own mystery to solve to find the Offenham terminus without plunging into the Avon. As the filmmakers would say, sealed off in a Midland Red cab, no-one can hear you scream. Note the bay number laid in stones in the road surface behind Miss Marple. For many years, Midland Red's carpenter for the production of timetable display cabinets and other non-bus furniture was the appropriately named Mr Tommy Wood. Did Tommy Steele do the metalwork? The search is still on for Tommy Fibreglass. *Peter Davey/ Bristol Vintage Bus Group*

D5B 3813 has loaded up in Edmund Street, Birmingham, and is making the right turn, today impossible, into Congreve Street. It is working the jointly operated Dudley Road corridor but will not be going all the way to Dudley, being a B85 as far as Spon Lane. This is another example of Birmingham City Transport drivers' exceptional ability to 'push' the bus in front! 2229, a Park Royal-bodied Leyland PD2 familiar on the Dudley Road for almost two decades, will follow the D5B all the way to Cape Hill. *Ken Jubb*

Midland Red buses on the X34/X35 services patrolled the English side of the border with Wales, speeding along the A49 between Hereford and Shrewsbury on journeys that took almost three hours each way. This was a spectacular run when viewed from a double-decker, taking in Leominster, Ludlow and the three Strettons among the regal scenery. Ludlow garage largely, although not exclusively, worked the X34 and X35 which varied from each other by serving different villages between the main towns. Ludlow's double-deck stock was supplemented in 1950s summers by three more transferred from Bearwood garage, with a fourth if necessary. Ludlow may sound like a soft billet for buses but, with few peak extras to allow some to lounge on the forecourt throughout the off-peak, they incurred the highest daily mileages in the fleet. D5B 3826, however, was having a day out from Shrewsbury's town services on 17 September 1955, loading in the bus station at Leominster on one of Shrewsbury garage's contributions to the X34/35. Leominster is a very pleasing quaint old town. *Peter Mitchell*

Kidderminster's D5B 3814 pulls into the Halesowen Library stop on its way to Bewdley on 21 May 1960. The D5 class provided a smooth and comfortable ride but their weight made them slow compared with other types in the fleet. Ford cars seem popular in Halesowen – one local on the right has splashed out on a two-tone version while the Ford on the left has an HA registration. *Peter Mitchell*

No.3826 on the previous page works a northbound X34. Here earlier D5 3546 is in Ludlow while serving a different selection of villages on a southbound X35. The bus is crossing Ludford Bridge over the River Teme, and behind is a British Railways lorry descending Lower Broad Street in low gear, its roar bouncing off the walls of the old houses. In addition to a fine castle, the town is full of Tudor timber-framed and Georgian red brick buildings and the tall pinnacled tower of the vast 15th century St Laurence's Church is visible from almost anywhere in Ludlow. *PM Photography*

Warwick may be the county town but it has been outgrown by its near neighbour, Leamington Spa. Despite the expansion, Leamington's Regency town centre is still much admired. D5B 3840 is on local service L58 although the slipping L may imply otherwise. *Transport Museum Wythall*

Redditch's first bus station was opened on 9 May 1953 and Ministry-imposed financial rules of the time meant it had to be constructed as cheaply as possible, shelters rendered surplus in the town being re-erected here. D5B 3797 leaves the bus station on 21 May 1960 pursued by sister bus 3851 on local service R22. The subsequent construction of the new town included impressive support for public transport with roads specifically for buses and a Transport Interchange, opened in 1973, directly connected to the Kingfisher shopping centre. The enlarged town was expected to fall into the West Midlands PTE area but, in the event, the latter's boundaries were not determined on travel patterns and Redditch remained outside. *Peter Mitchell*

If Redditch's bus station looked poverty-stricken, Market Harborough was surely worse. A boundary town between bus operators' territories, all those involved seemed reluctant to get a grip on the 'bus station', in reality a turning opportunity with tatty corrugated roof shelters. It could boast an impressive line of buses at times, however. In June 1961 Midland Red D5B 3861 is leader of the pack, followed by an S14, Bristols of United Counties and, in the far background, coaches of independent operators. *Transport Museum Wythall*

100 single-deckers with power operated doors were delivered from 1950, forming the S13 class. The prototype was no 3694, one of the previous tranche of 200 single-deckers, the remainder following in 1951-2 to become 3877-3975. Most were finished to a new dual-purpose standard with capacity reduced to 40 improved seats, suitable for longer bus services and sufficiently comfortable to help out the coach fleet at busy times. Those summer days seem a long way off here in a late 1950s winter as 3957, working the hourly 142 route from Redditch to Birmingham, crosses the Worcester & Birmingham Canal between Alvechurch and Barnt Green before skirting Bittell Reservoir. *Ken Jubb*

The busy Midland Red terminus in Birmingham's Bull Ring is already witnessing the beginning of change in August 1959; building demolition for the major reconstruction of the area has already taken the immediate background. Midland Red bought another 100 buses of outside manufacture to speed up vehicle replacement in 1952-3. The favoured supplier this time was Leyland; the resultant LD8 class (3978-4077) was very popular. Around a third of them were allocated to Birmingham's Digbeth garage and became a very familiar sight at the Bull Ring terminus. The powerful LD8s were ideal for the many services along country roads linking the Midlands towns such as the 159 to Coventry, about to be covered by 4035. The other two seen here were bound for Solihull, 4021 on the 152 travelling directly via Warwick Road and continuing on to Knowle while 4031 on the 154 would reach Solihull via Shirley and Blossomfield. 4031 has been restored by the 1685 Group at Wythall. *G H F Atkins archive/ S J Butler collection*

Bearwood Bus Station opened in January 1952 and hosted some very odd buses in its earliest days. The oldest of the four pre-war rear to underfloor engine conversions was 1591, rebuilt in 1941 and becoming known as the S1 in due course. It was the only one to retain a recognizable amount of its original body behind a much altered front end. It received these exaggerated mudwings in the 1941 rebuild. After an accident the front end was further rebuilt in 1952 as seen here. Air was taken in through grilles below the windscreens as part of an experimental heating system and the then new innovation of power doors. The front styling was arguably the tidiest ever evolved by Midland Red for an underfloor-engine bus but it sat uncomfortably with the pre-war design of the rest of the vehicle. *Gordon Davies*

LD8 4034 makes its way back to Birmingham from Earlswood along Norton Lane, Tidbury Green, in April 1957. *F W York/ Transport Museum Wythall*

Among Leamington's responsibilities was the 569 between Coventry and Balsall Common. Behind LD8 4049 at Pool Meadow Bus Station, Coventry, in March 1955 is the terrifying sight of a workman on a long ladder. The 569 service appeared to be overlooked when the agreement was made with the West Midlands Passenger Transport Executive, remaining with Midland Red after December 1973 despite being entirely within the imminent new West Midlands county. At that date WMPTE did not have an appropriate garage to run the service (Coventry not being added to the PTE until April 1974) so the anomaly was mopped up later. *G H F Atkins archive/ S J Butler collection*

IF YOU WISH TO TRAVEL BY ROAD

CONSULT—

THE FRIENDLY "MIDLAND RED"

LD8 4063 loads at Kidderminster Town Hall on its way from Stourport to Birmingham and is smartly turned out in its original livery with black wings and gold lining out. 4063 was a Bearwood bus for the first 12 years of its life. The Birmingham-Kidderminster services ran every 15 minutes in the early 1950s, half continuing to Bewdley (132 and 192) and half to Stourport (133). The powerful LD8s made light work of these hilly routes. The statue is of Rowland Hill, a native of Kidderminster and inventor of the postage stamp, creating the modern postal service with a cheap, prepaid charge. *Midland Red*

Platform staff around LD8 Leyland 4075 handle a passenger enquiry at Stafford station on 18 August 1965. Stafford garage was not a familiar home for LD8s and had received 4075 the previous month from Bearwood where it had operated since new in 1953. DD11 class Daimler Fleetline 5246 stands behind. *Andrew Willis*

Well rewarded car industry jobs in Coventry and Leamington caused staff retention problems over many years at Midland Red's two Leamington garages. There was a long history of buses and drivers being hired from other operators to work Leamington-based services with Midland Red providing the conductors, this practice spreading to other garages in the 1960s. An interesting development at the end of 1965 was the sale of two stored LD8 Leylands to G & G Coaches of Leamington. They were both former Leamington buses which were given plenty of work by their new owner on their traditional services. The pair, previously 4048 and 4055, are both seen here at Pool Meadow, Coventry, in November 1966 with S17 5625 and Coventry Corporation Daimler CVG6s. *T W Moore*

Midland Red in December 1935 took over two bus companies from Balfour Beatty and, unusually, ran them separately for the time being. The green buses of the Leamington and Warwick operation that had begun life as a tramway were only retained until 1 October 1937 but Stratford Blue was kept for many years as a separate operating company, also assisting on some Midland Red services. Leyland Tiger PS2 32 is seen working a Leamington to Coventry 517 journey in wintry conditions on Kenilworth Road, Coventry, in 1963. It is one of four outdated 1950 half-cab single-deckers that were rebodied with new double-deck Northern Counties bodies, re-entering service in 1963 and passing to Midland Red itself when Stratford Blue was fully absorbed on 1 January 1971. *T W Moore*

Redditch-allocated D7 4137 is seen in October 1957 alongside Tudor House at the junction of High Street and New Road, Bromsgrove. The Redditch – Bromsgrove service was often operationally linked with the Bromsgrove – Stourbridge route although this through facility was not always timetabled. The BMMO 'K' 8 litre engine had evolved into the 'KL' type in time for the D7 of which 350 were built between 1953 and 1957 (4078-4177, 4353-4552, 4723-4772). Early post-war buses had gained weight due to more robust construction, increased dimensions and additional features such as doors and heaters. Metro-Cammell was developing its new 'Orion' lightweight body to reverse the weight gain. The concept appealed to Midland Red and the D7 bodies were built by Metro-Cammell on 'Orion' principles while incorporating BMMO's ideas on styling. *F W York/ The Transport Museum, Wythall*

Stratford Blue provided the direct services between Stratford-upon-Avon and Evesham. Midland Red's service between the two was the 524, one of the company's most scenic routes taking around a half-hour longer via Mickleton, Chipping Campden and Broadway. Short workings between Stratford and Chipping Campden were numbered 525. Stratford Blue also ran some 525 journeys; it was important that these were marked in the timetable as initially Midland Red's Day Anywhere tickets could not be used on the buses of its subsidiary. A choice example at one time was the round journey departing at 1255 from Stratford, worked by Midland Red on Tuesdays, Wednesdays and Fridays and Stratford Blue on Mondays, Thursdays and Saturdays. Bromsgrove garage has supplied D7 4109 for this journey, loading in Chipping Campden's High Street. Campden's fine buildings are a legacy of a once-thriving wool trade. *Ken Jubb*

It is Saturday 25 May 1963 and the photographer has set off from Stafford with a Day Anywhere ticket on what would prove his best day for pictures of BMMO vehicles. Following lunch at Worcester, he has reached Chipping Campden at the other end of the network. The Cotswolds countryside may not be awesomely dramatic but the honey-coloured stone buildings enchant in the mellow rolling hills and their beauty draws in day-trippers and tourists from far and near. There were still plenty of passengers on offer in 1963 and Midland Red could still rustle up the staff for the duplicates needed to move them. S10 3661 reverses in Campden's High Street around the quaint branch of the Midland Bank, the driver of Bromsgrove's D7 4424 will no doubt do likewise. Half-timbered cars like the Morris Minor Traveller would fit better architecturally a few miles down the road! *Andrew Willis*

In contrast the driver of D7 4138 suffers the hazards of freezing weather on 2 February 1963. 4138 is in Lutterworth town centre, having arrived from Leicester. The blanked-off radiator helps to keep the engine warm but adds to the rather careworn look of the D7. There is an untidy mismatch of service numbers and the blind for the ultimate destination is in the lower 'via' box. *Peter Mitchell*

More snow on 2 February 1963, this time afflicting D7 4431 working service 491. The few journeys on service 491 comprised Midland Red's principal service between Banbury and Deddington's Market Place, these travelling via Adderbury. There were also three journeys each way on the Banbury to Hempton service which were extended to Deddington on Saturdays as service 502. City of Oxford Motor Services also served the Banbury to Deddington corridor. *Peter Mitchell*

Tamworth has seen massive housing and retail expansion since this photograph. Local road schemes have kept up with the developments, not to forget the diversion of the A5 onto a fast new dual carriageway. This is Bolebridge Street as it was in the days of D7s like 4420, crossing the River Anker just before it joins the River Tame on 5 September 1970. The impressive viaduct was completed in 1839 and carries the Birmingham to Derby rail line. *Peter Mitchell*

The frequent service between Leicester and Coventry was the 658 via Hinckley and Nuneaton but the X68 (at first 168 under the February 1928 service numbering) went the 'pretty way' via Sharnford and Wolvey to Coventry and onwards to Birmingham. Leicester's Southgate Street garage had the majority share in this, assisted by one working provided by Birmingham Digbeth. Southgate Street D7 4513 has a full load as it passes through Meriden, the alleged centre of England. The opening of the M69 in 1978 changed the character of the service completely, Leicester becoming linked to Coventry and Birmingham with motorway expresses. *Transport Museum Wythall*

D7 4522 picks up passengers in Warwick's impressive Market Square around 1960. The X90 between Coventry and Stratford would have to fly along when traffic delays in the major towns caused late running. It was not limited stop, however, so when it was decided from 1966 to reserve the X prefix for true limited stop services, it was renumbered to 590. *Transport Museum Wythall*

Cheltenham was for many years a most important centre for national coach operations so Worcester, the first major city to its north, also received plenty of coaches calling at its Croft Road stop. With the power station as backdrop, C3 4217 is working an Associated Motorways service (predecessor of National Express) from Cheltenham to Derby, briefly deviating from the old A38 north of Birmingham to serve Walsall on a journey just under five hours in length. The Ribble Leyland-bodied Royal Tiger behind will take the road through Kidderminster and Bridgnorth en route to Liverpool. 75 new Midland Red coaches were built for the 1954 season, replacing the 50 SLRs and theoretically sufficient to replace the 25 ONCs too. Business was booming, however, and the ONCs lived on. The newcomers comprised 63 C3 37-seaters, 4179-4241, for long distance services and 12 C4 touring coaches, originally seating only 32. *Lyndon W Rowe*

The C4s were downgraded in 1962, being replaced on cruises by 16 C3s rebodied as class CL3 with new, slightly longer (32 feet 7 inches), Plaxton 36-seat bodies. The CL3 rebodies wore an ivory livery in their first summer, lacking the very long association of high quality represented by the traditional red and black. Not only passengers' complaints caused them to be repainted for the next season, at least one tour driver found his party was initially refused entry to the reserved overnight hotel because the proprietor would not believe it was really a Midland Red coach! Midland Red maintained a strong reputation for its Coach Cruises which continued to grow through the 1960s. A seventeenth C3, 4203, was rebodied for the 1964 season. CL3 4229 is on the recently constructed St Martin's Circus in Birmingham. In the background is the remains of Worcester Street with the former Midland Red enquiry office still standing but about to be demolished to make way for new buildings, including the Rotunda. *D D Kirk*

The rebuilding of the company's Carlyle Works was completed in 1954, permitting bulk production of BMMO bodies. The first fruits were the 219 lightweight 'chassisless' S14 buses which entered service in the mid-fifties, the culmination of development work with earlier experimental vehicles. The neat looking buses (4178, 4254-4352, 4553-4600, 4651-4721) were considered by many to be far in advance of models on the open market – integral construction, rubber suspension (independent on the front) and disc brakes. BMMO also experimented with Hobbs automatic transmission in a number of S14s. Although the figure of 219 S14s sounds like a good period of standardisation, the joke was that no two were the same – building the bodies liberated BMMO's boffins! The obsession for minimising weight enabled the S14 to have single rear wheels, saving even more weight but giving a poor ride quality and inferior grip in slippery conditions. A few had twin rear wheels from new. 4310, seen at Callow End on 11 July 1964, was also not the normal S14 it appeared. The bus received an AEC AH470 engine and 5 speed synchromesh gearbox in 1957, not reverting to the usual BMMO 8 litre engine and David Brown 4 speed gearbox until 1966. It was retired in June 1967. Another S14 of the first series, 4347, ran with a Rootes TS3 two-stroke engine from new in 1956 until 1963. The S14s became the ideal candidates to work one-man operated services although some of the first batch, including 4310, were never converted. The introduction of driver only operation at Worcester was achieved on 23 March 1963, the process having been a painful experience for management, platform staff and passengers. Several years of negotiations had included strikes on several Saturdays in early 1962 when free replacement bus services were organized by the People's League for the Defence of Freedom and a frustrated Worcester Chamber of Commerce. *Peter Mitchell*

With major territorial operators United Counties to the north-east and City of Oxford to the south, Midland Red's Banbury garage squeezed between them with infrequent services east into Buckingham via Brackley or Croughton. The most direct route was the 494, taking 53 minutes in each direction. The Buckingham terminus was the Market Place; the Midland Red timetable showed connections to and from Aylesbury on United Counties route 346 whose green Bristol Lodekka is seen behind S14 4351. In the left background is the old gaol built in the style of a medieval castle. It now houses a museum instead of prisoners. *Peter Mitchell*

Banbury and Buckingham is linked by the A422. The 482 ran on Saturdays, diverting to serve Dadford and Stowe, famous for its school and landscape gardens. The road to Stowe meets the A422 at Water Stratford crossroads and is entered between these pillars that hint at the majestic buildings and follies to come. S14 4594 rejoins the A422 on 16 April 1960 after serving the two settlements which were also served on Tuesdays with the 495. *Peter Mitchell*

The A422 continues the other side of Banbury to Stratford-upon-Avon. Midland Red's Banbury operations were barely connected to the rest of the system, however, and followed the road only as far as the attractive stone village of Wroxton from where the 530 service then found its way to Tysoe. The latter is well spread and also of considerable appeal, evident in this view of S14 4692. The bus was new in 1958 and sent to Banbury garage in September 1961 after being made suitable for one-man operation. It spent the rest of the 1960s at Banbury before moving to Redditch. *Peter Mitchell*

The 480 was a very infrequent service linking Banbury with Shipston-on-Stour via Broughton and Brailes. In later years the 480 went onwards to complete a rather indirect way to Stratford-upon-Avon but, by the date of this picture, 27 September 1969, no journey actually travelled all the way between Banbury and Stratford, this departure being a short working to Sibford Gower, a photogenic village where S14 4349 is seen. 4349 had only recently joined Banbury's allocation but was the prototype one-man operated bus, as it would have been described at the time of its entry into service in 1956 at Hereford. The cab was fully enclosed, the driver entering at the rear, a degree of security soon thought unnecessary. *Peter Mitchell*

One size fits all. By the end of 1958, all single-decker buses were underfloor-engine BMMO single-deckers of 30 feet length, irrespective of loadings or road conditions. S14 4586 is passing through Staunton-on-Wye around 1964. It was new to Hereford in November 1956, made suitable for driver only operation five years later and withdrawn from service just short of a twelve year life. *Transport Museum Wythall*

Opposite top: Another trip towards the magic lands west of the River Severn! The 291 linked Kidderminster through Bewdley and across the hills to Tenbury Wells. S15 4636 passes through Wribbenhall and is about to cross the Severn using Thomas Telford's bridge of 1798 into the centre of Bewdley on 7 August 1962. The S15 was a variation of the S14, and 50 (4601-50) were produced in 1957. They reverted to twin rear wheels because they were intended, like most of the S13s, for longer distance work with 40 dual-purpose seats. They carried the black top coach livery enhanced with polished mouldings when new. *Peter Mitchell*

Opposite: The 291 and 132 services overlapped between Bewdley and Kidderminster. This scene in Bewdley on 23 September 1958 shows D7 4765 of Kidderminster garage at the picturesque starting point of the 132 in Load Street, Bewdley, waiting to depart for Birmingham. Bewdley and Stourport, both inland resorts on fine stretches of the river Severn, were popular destinations for day trips and short holidays throughout the Midland Red years, and Black Country garages would work extras on services to them at holiday weekends, providing a welcome break for the crews from their usual industrial journeys. This is a rainy day, too much of the wet stuff would cause the local residents to watch the Severn anxiously. The final batch of D7s, 4723-4772, were added to stock in 1957. The lightweight Metro-Cammell bodies were rather basic but achieved necessary fuel savings and meant that they were eager workhorses, well-liked by some Midland Red drivers who preferred its straightforward operation to the later D9. *Peter Mitchell*

The Dudley Road corridor in Birmingham continued to be jointly operated. One operator generally worked each service in the group but there were odd journeys worked by the other. Nearly all the journeys on the B82 to Bearwood were provided by Birmingham City Transport but Midland Red did operate a few, D7 4761 being photographed on 1 June 1968. For decades buses on the Dudley Road group set down their passengers here in Margaret Street, outside the impressive College of Arts and Crafts, and pulled around the corner into Edmund Street to load up – they were never transferred to the Bull Ring Bus Station opened in 1963. The D7s had a long career on the Dudley Road, agreement with the other operator (by then West Midlands PTE) to reschedule the services for 72-seaters not taking effect until January 1972. 4761 entered service in June 1957 at Oldbury garage where it remained for a life of over fifteen years before being converted to a towing vehicle, in which capacity it served until 1980. *Malcolm Keeley*

A tradition in the bus industry is for a retiring long-service driver to be pulled into the garage at the end of his final duty. Midland Red's photographer was called to Oldbury garage on 20 May 1963 when Driver Key was given this honour, having completed his final trip on the B86 - how many times must he have driven that road? There are a lot of inspector's caps in the picture, as well as drivers and clippies – a popular chap! Note the big key hanging from the catch of the opening windscreen. *Midland Red/ The Bus Archive*

Services and buses were absorbed from Leicester independents Kemp & Shaw and Boyer early in 1959. D7 4733 is working ex-Kemp & Shaw service X63 between Leicester and Derby bus station where it was seen on 8 April 1961. A Trent Leyland Atlantean is in the background, equipped with rear destination display. *Ken Swallow*

L40 was originally a Leamington local service but the number was later recycled to Leicester where it became one of the services to Birstall, the L30/L40 to Windmill Avenue and the L85 to Woodgate Drive. The L prefix gradually fell from use in Leicester, the L85 becoming 85 and the L30/40 rationalised as the 84. L40 was later reused in Leamington! Absorbing vehicles from acquired operators was extremely rare and added extra flavour to the Leicester operations for several years. Two Leyland PD2s with Leyland's own bodies were taken over from Kemp & Shaw. Prominent here is 4845 (JBC 989), a 1952 PD2/12 – Midland Red's LD8s carried a version of the manufacturer's standard body fitted to 4845, customised to meet the company's preferences. 4845 was an open-platform bus, however, and is seen alongside AD2 class AEC Regent/ Metro-Cammell 3151. The original concrete shelters of St Margaret's Bus Station were unattractive; the terminal was excellently rebuilt in the mid-1980s. *Transport Museum Wythall*

Midland Red's motorway coaches were kings of the road when the M1 opened. There was originally no speed limit and the coaches regularly cruised at over 80 mph, a major contrast to the 30 mph that had been the official speed limit for buses and coaches everywhere on older roads, irrespective of the speed limit for cars. Can anything instil more enthusiasm for this wonderful company than these four CM5Ts making short work of overtaking a private car with nothing challenging them in the outside lane? The second coach still has single headlights but the remainder have gained the extra security of twin headlights either mounted vertically or horizontally. *Midland Red*

The C5 coach was based on the lightweight S14 but the lantern windscreen and attractive interior disguised its origins well. The straight lines contrasted with the curved waistrails of the existing coaches. Midland Red introduced motorway express coaches between Birmingham and London on the very day the M1 opened in November 1959. For this new work the C5 was developed into the CM5 and CM5T (T for toilet) with turbocharging of the 8 litre engines and five-speed gearboxes. Here we have the tales of two unrelated Sinclairs who both developed C5s. Donald Sinclair's C5 family became one of the most iconic coach designs ever produced in the UK, more than capable of flattening the C5 battery-electric cars launched 25 years later by Sir Clive Sinclair. The glamour years of the C5 coaches could not last for ever but, fortunately, the straight lines permitted a very attractive looking dual-purpose service bus. Many were downgraded to this role, minus toilets and turbochargers where fitted, of course! 4778 is seen working from Banbury garage. *Peter Mitchell*

Birmingham proposed a new Civic Centre after World War One on a large site at the eastern end of Broad Street. Included in the development was the Hall of Memory, soon built to honour those who perished in the terrible slaughter and seen here behind the Standard car. Otherwise only the building later known as Baskerville House was built. This was not ready for occupation until 1940, and is the imposing structure behind D9 4868, seen in September 1960 when the bus was still fairly new. 4868 is turning right out of Broad Street into Easy Row whose interesting buildings, some dating from the 18th century, are just off camera to the right. These were demolished to make way for the hideous Paradise Circus development constructed within a huge traffic gyratory created here. The latter caused buses from Broad Street to turn left and, for a time, the streetscape was dominated by a deep chasm to allow pedestrian access over the traffic. The latest changes involve the extension of Midland Metro into Broad Street. The Hall of Memory and Baskerville House still survive and, if buildings could talk, no doubt would discuss wearily the changes they have seen. *Transport Museum Wythall*

Henley-in-Arden is a beautiful village with a long main street largely comprising timbered houses. New D9 4865 is seen on 21 May 1960 when Henley was famous for its home-produced ice creams. The Birmingham - Stratford upon Avon service 150 was a familiar number for many years to Brummies on a day out. The 150 became jointly operated with Stratford Blue from 1952 upon a frequency increase from hourly to half-hourly. *Peter Mitchell*

The Birmingham terminus for buses towards Halesowen and beyond was moved in December 1950 from Station Street to Navigation Street until the 1963 opening of the Bull Ring Bus Station. Passengers not travelling beyond Halesowen would hop from stop to stop to catch the first departure although hopefully platform staff or an inspector would give them the right answer. Here in Navigation Street, D9 4926 is on offer for Stourbridge but is not moving imminently while lurking behind is LD8 4008 bound for Bewdley on the 132. Between 1952 and 1959 on Easter, Whit and August bank holidays, 132/3s loaded in Worcester Street, opposite the company's enquiry office, on the wrong side of the street so the passengers had to step up from the roadway rather than the pavement. The buses then worked their way around via New Street to call at the normal loading stop in Navigation Street. *Roger Torode collection*

Opposite top: How we loved the first D9s, starting a long series that began at 4849. Inevitably with time they became ordinary workaday buses, sometimes looking a little uncared for. 4852, new in February 1960, travels along Deritend, Birmingham, en route to the Rover factory in Lode Lane, Solihull, on 17 October 1970. The A series (originally for Austin) for works services was first used on 8 January 1934. Larger dimensions meant a beefing up of certain components and, after the period of excessive weight cutting, the interior of the D9 was a relief! Despite being 30-feet long 72-seaters, they only weighed 7 tons 7.5 cwt so the new 10.5 litre engine provided generous performance. Driver fatigue was reduced by power steering, two pedal control and a semi-automatic gearbox. All very good but the side advertisement is a plea for more drivers. *Malcolm Keeley*

Opposite: We may recall Midland Red's premier routes running between the major towns or its buses battling through the cut-and-thrust of the big cities. In fact many Midland Red staff were quietly engaged on services drifting around the suburbs of small towns and this is a typical example. D9 5369 works a Banbury local at the junction of Timms Road and Harrowby Road on 27 September 1969. *Peter Mitchell*

1960 D9 4872 was still fairly new when seen at Stafford station, shortly to be transformed as part of the West Coast Main Line electrification. 4872 was notable for being the first of many fitted with an illuminated advertisement panel, following a trial installation on D5 3498. The long 865 service between Dudley and Stafford went via Walsall and was jointly worked with Walsall Corporation which was absorbed into West Midlands Passenger Transport Executive in 1969. When the PTE took over part of Midland Red in December 1973, the 865 was split into two overlapping sections. The PTE operated Dudley – Walsall - Cannock while Midland Red retained Walsall – Cannock - Stafford. 4872 remained at Dudley with the PTE and was withdrawn in January 1976 after over fifteen years at one of the most arduous garages. *Ken Jubb*

The driver could be forgiven for thinking he had wandered off-route at Norris Hill, near Ashby-de-la-Zouch. The date was June 1971 and D9 4897 is about to be transferred away from Swadlincote garage where it had operated since delivery in December 1960. *Peter Mitchell*

Opposite top: BMMO's highly innovative D10 underfloor-engine double-deckers, built in 1960-1, were easily dismissed by the uninitiated who presumed them to be rear-engine buses. The first D10, 4943, began road trials in July 1960, entering passenger service in January 1961. It is seen here on a very early passenger journey at Pool Meadow, Coventry, with an S6, by then one of the company's oldest vehicles, providing a contrast in the background. At the May 1962 Annual General Meeting of BMMO, Chairman John Spencer Wills announced the future vehicle plans. On the double-deck front, he advised that 50 Daimler Fleetlines would supplement a further 150 D9s to be built – these 200 buses became 5245-94 and 5296-5445. He referred to the two D10s, 4943-4, noting that they were working satisfactorily in ordinary service and the design was likely to feature in a future production programme. In the event, no more D10s were built. *T W Moore*

Opposite: BMMO S15 5053 is at Rugeley Post Office on 26 October 1963. Single-deck production had recommenced in 1962 to begin in earnest the replacement of the early post-war fleet. Initially proposed were 100 BMMO single-deckers comprising more S14s and dual-purpose S15s, 50 of each. Only 48 of the dual-purpose S15s were actually built, numbered 5045-92. *Peter Mitchell*

Above: 1962 S15 5077's premier days as a dual-purpose bus are gone and it is clearly in need of some tender loving care as it works a Rugby local on Yates Avenue, Newbold Glebe estate on 4 August 1969. The 1957 batch of S15s were converted to one-man operation in 1965-6 but just one of the second batch of S15s was so treated. The rest required conductors for their relatively short lives, only running for around ten years and taken out of service in 1972-3. *Peter Mitchell*

The bus-seated vehicles began, as expected, with 5095 in spring 1962. A recent increase in permitted length from 30 to 36 feet for single-deckers allowed two extra rows of seats, taking capacity up to 52. The company decided to build the 50 buses to the new dimensions with 5095 as the prototype, retaining the 8 litre engines and constant-mesh gearboxes of the smaller S14s they were originally intended to be. The new type was classified S16, this is 5097 on 8 September 1963 on Mill Bank, Wellington, which today looks rather different with old structures on the right-hand side replaced by new housing. The S16s were arguably underpowered but a further batch was produced in 1964 (5512-45), using up stocks of 8 litre engines and four-speed constant-mesh gearboxes removed from C5s upgraded to five-speed. *Peter Mitchell*

5186 crosses the River Avon at Ryton-on-Dunsmore in June 1966, having commenced its journey at Shrewsbury. The driver has battled through the Black Country, Birmingham and Coventry; he is now on the A45, relieved to leave the congestion behind at last and hoping for a clear run to Northampton. Production of BMMO buses could not keep up with the replacement of the early post-war fleet from 1962 onwards so 100 Leyland Leopards bodied by Weymann or Willowbrook to the new 36 feet length, 5145-5244, were ordered to assist single-deck renewals. 5186 was one of twenty LS18s whose Willowbrook bodies were finished to 'black roof' dual-purpose 48-seat specification as class LS18A and ideal for services like this. *T W Moore*

Allesley retains much of the feel of a country village but is actually an outer suburb of Coventry. 53-seat bus specification LS18 5198 powers between characterful properties in September 1973. Three months later the 159 Coventry – Birmingham service and 5198 would pass to the West Midlands PTE.
T W Moore

LS18 Leyland Leopard/Willowbrook 5244 has just squeezed under the low railway bridge in Station Road, Old Hill, on 12 June 1972. The routes under this bridge would be taken over by West Midlands PTE in December 1973 so it was that operator who faced the problem of the replacement Leyland Nationals not being able to get under the bridge due to their rear roof pods. The road was therefore lowered under the bridge, an interesting exercise as a canal runs alongside. Leyland announced the 'podless' National around the time the works were completed! 5244, along with other LS18s at Stourbridge garage, would join former Digbeth LS18s at the PTE's ex-Birmingham City Transport garage in Yardley Wood which had a long history of running Leylands.
Peter Mitchell

The production of D9 double-deckers was supplemented by 50 Alexander-bodied Daimler Fleetlines, 5245-5294, known as the DD11 class. Midland Red had been cautious about rear engines since its experiments with such vehicles in the 1930s and the Fleetline order was seen as a major coup for Daimler, one of the major employers in Coventry. Appropriately this is a busy Coventry scene at Pool Meadow on Whit Monday (30 May) 1966. The 159 was largely operated by Digbeth garage but Sheepcote Street also helped out, on this occasion providing DD11 5254. The bus alongside is a Daimler CVG6 of Coventry Corporation whose bus fleet was forced into West Midlands PTE in 1974. *Andrew Willis*

BMMO produced another 150 D9s, 5296-5445, beginning in 1963 but taking until 1966 to get them all on the road. 5297 works local service C87 along Belvoir Road, Coalville, opposite Owen Street. The street is eerily empty but these are days long before Sunday trading became permitted, this being Whit Sunday (29 May) 1966. *Peter Mitchell*

The river loops around a wealth of fine buildings in Welford-on-Avon including many half-timbered thatched cottages. D9 5380 works an ex-Stratford Blue service from Evesham in the early 1970s and, having travelled the flood prone road south of the river from Barton and Bidford, approaches the Bell Inn in the centre of Welford-on-Avon. The inn is still in use but much of the greenery seen here has disappeared through gradual gentrification. *Transport Museum Wythall*

The S16 was soon succeeded by the much more popular S17. They looked very similar but were quite different under the floor. The S17 enjoyed the 10.5 litre engine, two pedal control and semi-automatic gearbox recently introduced with the D9 double-decker. The extra power was very useful here as 5492 of Stourbridge garage climbs from Cradley towards the A458 main road through Colley Gate on 12 June 1972. *Peter Mitchell*

BMMO 36-footers had poor lock so S17 5511 of Wellington garage makes a tight fit at Astley Abbotts on service 912 from Bridgnorth under a threatening sky on 25 June 1971. Having another employee on the platform blocking your view to the nearside wouldn't help! *Peter Mitchell*

We return to High Street, Bromsgrove, previously seen on page 43. The date is 9 May 1971, around the time Alcester Road in the background was renamed Stratford Road. The Coach & Horses has been demolished and a Tesco supermarket is nearing completion on the site. Emphasising the massive size of Midland Red's route network, the X72 took almost three hours to travel from Birmingham to Gloucester and standard double-deck buses were familiar for many years. The X72/73 Birmingham – Gloucester/ Cheltenham services would soon be shortened to operate south of Worcester only and renumbered 372/3. S17 5557 has suffered fire damage, being repaired in early 1970 with this replacement roof in the peaked style used on the S23 class. 5557 belonged to Bromsgrove garage which became an early victim of the closure programme, finishing on the last day of 1971. The garage was sold but soon repurchased, being re-opened on 3 December 1973 to take on Worcestershire work from garages passed to West Midlands PTE, finally closing in 1983. *Peter Mitchell*

Chipping Campden and its surrounding villages were served from Evesham by two groups of routes, the 392/3/8 via Badsey and Bretforton, and the 523/4/6 via Broadway and Willersey. S17 5559 is seen on 19 August 1972 in beautiful Willersey, nestling at the foot of the North Cotswold ridge. One village, Ebrington, used to be the butt of humour for Chipping Campden people who called them Yubberton Yawnies. They particularly mocked the inferior height of the village's church tower, a typical joke being the alleged placing of manure by Ebrington locals at the foot of it to make it grow. Size was evidently everything even then! *Peter Mitchell*

Long-established services to Kidderminster were extensively revised on 18 November 1972, including an end to the 882/3/5 group of services from Wolverhampton. The 885 ran all the way to Kidderminster. The 882 operated between Wolverhampton and Stourbridge only, the combined 882/885 providing a 30-minute headway between those two towns, improved to 15 minutes on Saturdays. The 883 also ran between Wolverhampton and Kidderminster but followed a rural route via Kinver and Kingsford, providing only 3 or 4 departures each day. 1964 S17 5593, allocated to Kidderminster, is seen in Drakelow (between Kingsford and its home town) on 23 June 1971. *Peter Mitchell*

Alight here for trains to Paris? Sir Edward Watkin was involved with several railway companies, not least the Manchester, Sheffield and Lincolnshire Railway which later became the Great Central Railway. He decided to build another main line to London, intended to provide the fastest journey times between the existing railway in northern England and the capital. The London Extension was opened to passengers in 1899 and was the last UK main line built in the steam era, Rugby Central being one of the new stations. Watkin also supported the construction of a rail tunnel under the English Channel to allow goods produced in the north of England to be distributed to European markets by rail. There is no real evidence that Watkin planned to put the two great projects together but, if railway history had been different, perhaps you could have transferred from Midland Red buses to GCR main line trains to destinations beyond London Marylebone. S17 5623 passes Rugby Central on 13 August 1966, the station closed in May 1969 under railway rationalisation. *Peter Mitchell*

If Enid Blyton had written 'Five go down a Coalmine' then she may have invented a town named Coalville. The real Leicestershire town of Coalville is on the fringe of a pretty area but also did what it said on the label. S17 5738 is working the C70 at Stanton under Bardon on 23 March 1972. The C70 ran according to colliery requirements to Ellistown, Bagworth and Desford collieries. 5738 belonged to a final batch of S17s built in 1965-6 taking fleet numbers 5675 to 5773 (5722-4 were completed as prototypes for further dual-purpose buses). One-man operation using 36-feet single-deckers began with S17s from late 1966. The rebuilding of D7 4088 to a mobile workshop occurred as the o.m.o. conversion programme was stepped up considerably from November 1968, extending to double-deckers. The workshop toured garages to do all the necessary modifications so scarce drivers were not needed to ferry S17s, LS18s and Fleetlines to and from Central Works. Relatively few S16s were converted due to their manual gearboxes. *Peter Mitchell*

Midland Red's motorway services were very successful and warranted coaches to the new permitted length of 36 feet to obtain more seats. The CM5 motorway coaches were replaced in 1965-6 by 29 CM6 vehicles numbered 5646-5674. CM6T 5664 with a full load leaves Pool Meadow, Coventry, completely unrecognisable today. On its roof is an anti-nationalisation poster, dating this picture to 1967. Actually Midland Red had been part state-owned for many years due to railway shareholdings. The controlling interest, however, continued to be held by British Electric Traction until it sold its bus interests to the state in November 1967, leading to the creation of the National Bus Company. *T W Moore*

Midland Red began buying Leyland Leopards for its coach fleet in 1965, no 5777 being seen in August of that year at Whitley in Coventry. It is one of 49 with Duple 49-seat bodies that formed the LC7 class. A 50th Leopard, 5823, had a Plaxton touring coach body to become the solitary LC8; it was the first of very many Plaxton-bodied Leopards for the company. *T W Moore*

The last BMMO buses, 5849-5991, were single-deckers with rather confusing seating qualities. Previous dual-purpose buses lacked adequate luggage capacity for coach services so a new designation was the semi-coach. These were vehicles used on bus services during the week with sufficient luggage space to perform weekend coach duties, allowing coaches underused on weekdays to be disposed of. 5849-78 were S21 class semi-coaches, followed by 5879-5915, S22 dual-purpose buses. Midland Red was forever adjusting its local services. By the time of this 31 July 1971 picture of S22 5909 providing a comfortable ride around Sutton Coldfield, the S63 was a circular service, numbered S62 in the opposite direction. Commencing at the traditional BCT terminus near the junction of Sutton Road and Chester Road, the circular went via Boldmere, Sutton centre, Mere Green, Streetly and New Oscott, returning to the Chester Road terminus. This is Sutton Oak Road. *Peter Mitchell*

With 'TOWN SERVICE' occupying the top blind, 5898's ultimate destination on 28 June 1971 is shown on the lower blind and is one of the oddest on the network. It reads 'BEACONSIDE (16 M.U.)'. Stafford's local services included two cross-town services between Rickerscote in the south and Beaconside in the north. Many of the latter went to the main gates of the RAF maintenance unit which was a significant employer in Stafford. 5898 is a 1968 dual-purpose S22 and, like almost every member of the class, relied on forced air ventilation. 5898 differed by having a different style of flush window glazing - introduced as standard later that year on S23s, although being service buses the latter employed sliding ventilators rather than forced air. *Peter Mitchell*

5916 passes through the attractive village of Drayton on 27 September 1969, where the Roebuck Inn is still in business, on its way back to Banbury from Wroxton. The usual service through here was the 530 but the 531 was a once a day variation to Wroxton's Abbey Gates with an additional journey on Saturday nights. BMMO production concluded with 76 S23 bus-seated service buses (5916-91). 5916 had been new at the end of 1968 but the gradual loss of staff meant it took until mid-1970 for all the S23s to be completed. 5916 spent its first two years working from Banbury garage. *Peter Mitchell*

This attractive spot is Charlton, between Pershore and Evesham, being served by S23 5930 on 14 August 1970. The last BMMO buses were withdrawn from normal service early in 1981; the final four survivors were all based at Warwickshire garages and included 5930 by then moved to Rugby. *Peter Mitchell*

S23 5940 is working the infrequent service from Leicester operated on Saturdays to Medbourne, seen here on 8 May 1971. *Peter Mitchell*

The B39 was one of Midland Red's more obscure urban services, the B prefix in this case denoting the one and only Brierley Hill local. There were four journeys, twelve minutes in each direction, every two hours in the off-peak on Mondays to Saturdays between Brierley Hill and Upper Pensnett estate. This is S23 5958 in Tennyson Street, Upper Pensnett on 12 June 1972. *Peter Mitchell*

This delightful view shows 1966 DD12 class 6015 on Stratford Road, Harvington, bound for Norton and Evesham. Traffic can still enter Harvington using this road today but it is no longer possible to exit the village in the direction being taken by 6015. Shrinking BMMO production saw the Alexander-bodied Daimler Fleetline become the standard double-deck bus from 1966. Midland Red built up a fleet of around 300 Fleetlines but they are rare in preservation, happily 6015 survives at Wythall. *Transport Museum Wythall*

The first use of prefix letters occurred when Worcester's trams last ran on 31 May 1928 and replaced by Midland Red buses the following day. The agreement between the Corporation and Midland Red was considered a good model; 'Worcester Agreement' terms became convenient shorthand for bus operators all over the UK. Midland Red's reluctance to take delivery of double-deck buses in the 1970s makes it surprising to remember that garages were still being rebuilt to take more of them as late as 1967. As well as major work at Rugby, improvements at Worcester's Padmore Street garage at last allowed the regular use of double-deckers on a revised network of city services. Fifteen new DD12 class Alexander-bodied Daimler Fleetlines, 6046-55 and 6092-6, were delivered to Worcester by the end of the year. Here are three DD12s in Angel Place with the Midland Red clock gracing the company's enquiry office, and the impressive old shelters then still numerous around the city. *Midland Red/ The Bus Archive*

Midland Red's official photographer visited Worcester on 22 May 1968 to photograph traffic conditions in the city, including the previous picture and also make use of this vantage point above Worcester Bridge. DD12 6047 is struggling through the traffic. Newport Street bus station is to the right of the photographer and would occasionally be flooded by the River Severn after inclement weather. *Midland Red/ The Bus Archive*

It now seems odd to see a Midland Red bus as recent as DD12 Daimler Fleetline 6060 operating under trolleybus wires but it happened for several years. These are Walsall Corporation's wires in High Street, Bloxwich, in October 1967. The Walsall system would run for another three years – the final year under West Midlands PTE. 6060 is working the 865 Stafford-Walsall-Dudley service, jointly worked with motorbuses of Walsall Corporation. Walsall's older buses only had two route number tracks and showed 65, interestingly displayed by 6060. *F W York/ Transport Museum Wythall*

Leicester local service L84 ran hourly to Downing Drive, infilling between other Midland Red services along Uppingham Road to and from points further afield. DD12 Fleetline 6088 is on Uppingham Road, by Spencefield Lane, and is followed on 16 August 1969 by an S21 working a long-distance service thanks to its semi-coach credentials. Leicester City Transport also ran in the vicinity but its buses to and from the city centre travelled via London Road. The L84 was a useful link for Downing Drive residents with the city end of Uppingham Road which was bustling with shops. *Peter Mitchell*

Midland Red private parties included all sorts of people over the years from transporting the Australian cricket team to providing five coaches for the Red Army Ensemble, although one cannot imagine the latter hiring coaches of any other colour! The Gravelly Hill Interchange, more popularly known as Spaghetti Junction, was opened on 24 May 1972 and again Midland Red coaches scored a first. VIPs enjoyed a tour of the complex Interchange and were then conveyed to a civic reception at Birmingham's Council House by twelve coaches contracted from Midland Red. This view in Victoria Square shows seven of them stretching along Colmore Row, led by LC11 class Leyland Leopard/Plaxton 6228 (WHA 228H). This could well have been the last big private hire handled by traditional Midland Red coaches as all the decades of goodwill was about to be thrown away by the National Bus Company imposing its dirt-prone white livery and transferring coach business to its Central Activities group. *Malcolm Keeley*

There were several Midland Red services from Bilston that followed different routes to Dudley. Daimler Fleetline 6286 was three months old when seen at Bilston station on 10 April 1971. The area looks rundown; Bilston's last passenger trains ceased in 1972 upon the closure of the Birmingham Snow Hill to Wolverhampton Low level line. Midland Metro now follows the abandoned alignment and the quality of public transport infrastructure in central Bilston has been improved beyond recognition. Midland Red's later Alexander-bodied Fleetlines additionally had centre exits, infrequently used, and formed the DD13 class. 6286 belonged to the final batch which had Alexander's redesigned front panel that reminds you of somebody trying to fit a whole banana lengthways into his mouth. *Peter Mitchell*

A choice of hostelries in Eardisley, Herefordshire, with the New Inn and the Tram Inn; the latter's sign showing how it got its name. The slow entry into service of the S23s meant replacement of S14s dropped behind schedule. To replace ageing S14s as quickly and cheaply as possible, Midland Red decided a Ford was affordable. Its purchase of 100 Ford buses bodied by Plaxton over the winter of 1970-1, including 6347 seen on 25 June 1971, was a massive investment by the company in its rural bus services. Plaxton no doubt found the big order useful during the off-season for coach bodies. They were followed by a further 40 in two batches delivered in National Bus Company livery in 1972-4. *Peter Mitchell*

The 411 operated on Hereford's market days, Wednesday and Saturday, between the city and Fromes Hill although in earlier days it ran as far as Worcester. One of the settlements served en route was Yarkhill where Ford 6383 passes St John the Baptist Church on 26 June 1971. The church bells have been refurbished and continue to ring out over the River Frome. *Peter Mitchell*

Ford 6321 is seen at the Market Place, Rugby in March 1971 on one of several routes running between Coventry and Rugby serving different villages.
T W Moore

An extremely tight junction for the driver of Ford 6363 in Elmley Castle on 17 May 1973. Elmley Castle was then served by the 385, 401 and 404 which sounds generous but all were very infrequent, linking small but pretty villages under the gaze of Bredon Hill between Evesham and Pershore. There is a long history of tourism in the Vale of Evesham with the attraction of the villages being supplemented each spring by blossom tours of the orchards. Hopefully the Midland Red drivers knew where they were going as, in the days before television, bored young villagers would entertain themselves by turning round direction signs to confuse the visitors. *Peter Mitchell*

A former Stratford Blue Leyland PD3 is seen at Abbot's Salford on 14 April 1972, the Midland Red subsidiary company having been fully absorbed on 1 January 1971. As part of the administrative economies, Stratford and Midland Red's Evesham garage began to share the same local management while Stratford Blue's small garage at Kineton became responsible to Banbury garage. It is notable that Midland Red, having changed its mind after long experience of FEDD buses, continued to favour rear entrances on its front-engine double-deck buses. Its operating subsidiary Stratford Blue, however, followed a national trend towards the front-entrance layout on thirty-foot long double-deckers, allowing the driver to take some responsibility for loading while the conductor handled the greater number of fares. Stratford Blue's services could not be described as crush-load urban so its conductors were rarely under great pressure. Its territory, however, was very attractive so moving the entrances and staircases to the front was unfortunate for lower deck riders whose forward vision was considerably hampered. Most of the 15-strong Stratford Blue Leyland PD3 fleet received Midland Red livery but all were sold to Isle of Man Road Services in 1971-2. 2008 was one of Stratford Blue's last pair of PD3s to be delivered and dated from 1966. Willowbrook built the 73-seat body. It served the Isle of Man until 1983. *Peter Mitchell*

The Colour Supplement

This is the notoriously tight turning space at Malvern Wells terminus where the Tilling-Stevens forward entrance double-decker is already facing towards Birmingham in the 1920s. The long run through Worcester, Bromsgrove and Rubery took just under three hours in each direction! Improved buses allowed timings to be speeded up from 12 January 1929. The 144, as the service became under the 1928 renumbering, then took 2 hours 20 minutes each way, a timing that lasted for decades. Even on the quicker timing, the 'Myrtle' tea rooms across the road were no doubt very welcome after the journey. Myrtle is no longer in business. *Transport Museum Wythall*

Dunchurch was once an important market town on the London to Holyhead road, busy as a stopping point for stagecoach passengers, but the modern world has passed it by. Rugby, three miles to the north, has outgrown it and the motorways take the through traffic. The centre is now a conservation area. Going back a century, the conductor stands proudly alongside HA 3536, a 1926 SOS FS, one of the first forward control buses in the fleet. *Transport Museum Wythall*

Coventry had many quaint corners but much was destroyed in World War Two. This is a reminder of Coventry before the devastation with 1927 SOS 'Queen' HA 3684 and companions loading at Greyfriars Green, a major centre for Midland Red before the opening of Pool Meadow bus station in October 1931. *Transport Museum Wythall*

Opposite top: The development of bus services within and radiating from Leicester was a major ambition for the company in the 1920s. 1920 Tilling-Stevens TS3 OE 6187 is seen in Melton Mowbray, famous for hunting and pork pies and many miles from the company's original heartland around Birmingham. *Transport Museum Wythall*

Opposite: 1924 SOS Standard HA 2377 on a return journey to Leicester. *Transport Museum Wythall*

This publicity image shows 1939 ONC FHA 401 leaving the company's combined coach station and garage in Digbeth, Birmingham. The ONC has its sliding roof open and is wearing its original livery, all known colour photographs of ONCs show the red and black livery adopted as standard after World War Two. *Transport Museum Wythall archive*

Opposite top: Welcome aboard. 1948 S8 3274 is loading on local service S11 at Barker Street, Shrewsbury, with Rowley's House in the background. The steep steps are caused by the underfloor engine, inevitable on a Midland Red single-decker in 1963, such a high floor and narrow entrance is unimaginable nowadays. It is a tempting proposition nevertheless although the lady is resisting, evidently not wishing to travel to the site of the Battle of Shrewsbury. All Battlefield journeys ran to Harlescott Grange as service S10 from June 1964. *Transport Museum Wythall*

Opposite: The Malvern local services reached their peak around 1956, requiring a dozen buses. 1949 S9 3384 does not have any trafficators so the driver hand signals his departure from Great Malvern Post Office, nestling below the Malvern Hills – the whole wonderful confection looking as if it could slide away eastwards at any moment but, of course, it is still there today. Cars include a very attractive Morris Minor convertible. The bus conductor stands on the entrance steps. Unusually the spray painting has claimed 3384's polished windscreen surround by the time of this picture, only a few months before its withdrawal in September 1965. Malvern local services were renumbered into the M series in January 1935, allowing 3xx numbers to be used for further country services in the Worcester area. The M26 in its original form was numbered 376. Withdrawal of post-war buses began in 1961. Some buses would be selected for further service and overhauled, meaning the last examples of classes could outlive their compatriots considerably. A single example of the first post-war class, S6 3023, survived into 1965. The huge intake of new, larger buses between 1963 and 1966 eliminated most of the pre-lightweight fleet. Midland Red's single-deck fleet in passenger service at the beginning of 1967 contained only four of this style of bus (two S9s and two S12s) and only four S13s. *Transport Museum Wythall*

D5 3475 at Newport Street, Worcester, promises a glorious long run with its increasingly rare open rear platform providing welcome ventilation on this warm evening in the late summer of 1963. It will take 50 minutes to reach Kidderminster and then a further 30 minutes to Stourbridge. Behind 3475 is S13 3904 loading on the 312 to Lickhill via Stourport. Modernisation of the double-deck fleet was moving as fast as the single-deckers. The GD6s were gone by 1962 and the AD2s by 1963. The last double-deck heavyweights, the D5Bs and LD8s, were retired in 1967. *Transport Museum Wythall*

In 1953 the Leamington area received a large quantity of new LD8 class Leyland PD2s. They were perfectly suited to the fast roads and the terrain, often having to recover time lost by congestion around the tourist magnets. They became a familiar sight for many years in Stratford-upon-Avon's bus station which occupied land leased from Flower's brewery surrounding the Red Lion public house. LD8 4056 awaits departure with Stratford Blue 27, a Leyland of similar specification, lurking behind. Buses ceased to use the Red Lion site and moved on-street as bus service deregulation approached in 1986. *Roland Box*

A nostalgic view of buses working in Hereford. BMMO D5B 3784 is leaving the bus station and passing the company's enquiry office for the city. S14 4302 is in the background. The bus station looked quite different when new because the cinema had not been built. *Transport Museum Wythall*

The handsome S15s never looked right after losing their black roofs on demotion from dual-purpose to ordinary bus duties. Originally built for long-distance services and occasional use as a coach, 4649 is now on the 13 minute journey between Hereford city centre and Three Elms. *Ken Jubb*

Opposite top: Cradley Heath had its own Midland Red garage, opened on Forge Lane opposite the railway station on 27 March 1939. In 1946 it became a centralised dock serving the western area garages. The special status encouraged the operating of various single-deck prototypes and experimental vehicles from Cradley Heath in the 1950s including the solitary LA 3977 and S12s with trial AEC, Leyland and BMMO engines from mid-1951. Prototype S13 3694, seen here in Lower High Street, Cradley Heath, was a familiar sight for many years. 3694 was Midland Red's first thirty feet long bus and the company was proud to place it on the road on the very first day buses to that length became legal, 1st June 1950. The body by Brush had 44 seats to bus standard, although the heavy investment in brightwork promised more luxury than it actually contained. *Transport Museum Wythall*

Opposite: S13 3904 has arrived at Tan Lane Schools at Stourport on a lunchtime school journey from the Walshes Estate on 21 September 1965. This was a standard S13 new in 1952, finished to dual purpose standard and seating only 40. The dual purpose S13s were repainted in the black top coach livery around 1956 but many reverted to all-over red in their final years when they were considered too old to assist the coach fleet. *Roland Box*

The CM5T motorway coaches became arguably Midland Red's most famous design, giving the company immense operational and technical prestige. The seating capacity was reduced from 37 to 34 as the "T" indicated a toilet compartment, previously a rare feature on a British coach as comfort breaks were usual. A rather delightful, albeit antiquated, feature of these machines was the use of wooden route boards on each side above the windows. 4805 leads a duplicated departure along Digbeth in this evocative view. While the Birmingham motorway coaches featured toilets, the Coventry ones, introduced on 1 September 1960, did not. The latter were supplied from Nuneaton garage, a good example of the company ensuring outer garages enjoyed some premier work. Logically the Coventry service was soon extended to and from Nuneaton. *T C Bassindale/ Transport Museum Wythall*

Opposite: 5077 was one of the second batch of S15s produced in 1962 which differed in minor ways from the 1957 originals. 5077 moved to Malvern garage in May 1963, staying there for around seven years. Carrying red and black dual-purpose livery, it is working the 477 through Wyche Cutting to Ledbury via Colwall on 24 September 1965. Many journeys on the 477 then ran all the way from Malvern to Hereford but the route was split at Ledbury from 16 March 1968, the Ledbury-Hereford section becoming service 476. *Roland Box*

Midland Red went through a very confused period with fleet name and number transfers around 1970. The fleet number of 1962 D9 5008 is in the traditional style but above the front lower saloon passenger window. The take-up of illuminated advertisement spaces was poor; most became disused or were removed. 5008 is seen in Colmore Circus, Birmingham, on 6 April 1972 and would prove a short-lived D9, being withdrawn in May 1973 and thus not passing to the West Midlands Passenger Transport Executive in December. *Malcolm Keeley*

Opposite top: Just around the corner from Hereford's bus station is 1957 D7 4750 which operated from the city's garage for almost all its 15-year life. *Ken Jubb*

Opposite: The Birmingham-Dudley-Wolverhampton corridor had frequent Midland Red services, some journeys being extended to and from Stafford. 1963 D9 5326 is seen in Wolverhampton at the Cleveland Road terminus. Wolverhampton's transport department was very keen on trolleybuses for several decades and their wires can be seen clearly. Wolverhampton's last trolleybuses finished in 1967 and the transport department was swallowed into West Midlands PTE two years later. To the right is a Midland Red parcels agent. The carriage of parcels began as part of the Black Country tram facilities and was extended to Midland Red buses in 1915; the trams and Midland Red then being under the common ownership of British Electric Traction. For a time the parcels service was so successful that Midland Red branched into goods vehicles, some painted in the liveries of major customers. Eventually heavy items were taken over by Pickfords but smaller parcels continued to be carried between appointed agents by Midland Red buses to produce extra revenue. Parcels carriage ended on 2 May 1980 due to rising costs and falling income. *Roland Box*

It was always a pleasure to see the Midland Red buses lined up and loading along Evesham's High Street, often joined by buses belonging to Stratford Blue or Bristol. S17 5466 is nearest to the camera, the double-decker is D9 4862 while S14 4707 is the third of the trio. The timetable cases have been modernised to fibreglass since Miss Marple looked at them on page 77. *Barry le Jeune*

Coventry's Priory Street lost its northern end when the central ring road was constructed. Most of Priory Street's traffic then became buses and coaches leaving the city's Pool Meadow Bus Station. To the left is the legendary source of refreshments, the huge CAFÉ lettering painted on the roof and the multi-faced clock mounted on a tower being visible right across the bus station. CM6T 5662 carries the maroon roof colour that briefly replaced black from May 1967 before coaches became all-red from November 1970. National Bus Company white was imposed from 1972. *Transport Museum Wythall*

It must be Easter judging by the egg related promotional advert in the windscreen of ex-Stratford Blue 2058, a 1965 Leyland PSU3/3RT with Duple 49-seat coachwork, seen alongside the Red Lion at Stratford. 2058 looks like a Midland Red LC7 but differs as the more conservative-minded Stratford Blue preferred a manual gearbox to the LC7's semi-automatic. This coach later worked from Evesham and Wellington. *Ken Jubb*

The M5 opened in the Midlands on 20 July 1962 south of Lydiate Ash and Midland Red immediately introduced hourly Birmingham-Worcester express service X44 via Selly Oak and the motorway, reducing the journey time between the two cities from 93 minutes to 50, faster than the existing rail services. A variant, the X43, was introduced via Bearwood when the M5 was extended northwards to Quinton and beyond. The initial vehicles were the famous BMMO CM5 motorway coaches, those for the Worcester service not being equipped with toilets. The replacing CM6 coaches for the Birmingham-Worcester service also did not have toilets. The CM6s did not have a long life, all being withdrawn in 1972-4. Those on the X43/44 Birmingham-Worcester services were transferred to other work in the spring of 1972, initially being replaced by 1965 LC7 class Duple-bodied Leyland PSU3 Leopards converted to driver-only bus duties as class CM7A. These were withdrawn in January 1973 and sold to City of Oxford Motor Services. No 5784 is seen near the Kings Head, Bearwood, during the brief reign of the CM7A; note the yellow destination blinds. Bus-grant Leopards subsequently became the norm on the Worcester expresses. *Ken Jubb*

Bearwood Bus Station had seen many unusual vehicles in Midland Red livery over the years, not least the many prototype BMMO buses operated by Bearwood garage. Secondhand 1960 Weymann 'Fanfare'-bodied Leyland Leopards, however, were most unexpected. Five Leopards were bought from Sheffield in mid-1970 and ran for up to a year, most of them from Bearwood, no 6259 (6173 WJ) being seen here. The final BMMO buses had just been delivered and the Leopards helped out until the first 100 Fords arrived. *Ken Jubb*

A cheery goodbye from Bearwood!
Transport Museum Wythall, courtesy John Harris

Bibliography

Midland Red Bus Garages by Malcolm Keeley, published by Ian Allan 2013
Midland Red Style by Roger Torode & Malcolm Keeley, published by Capital Transport 2011
Working Days Midland Red by Malcolm Keeley, published by Ian Allan 2008
Stratford Blue by Robert L Telfer, published by Tempus 2003
Midland Red volumes 1 & 2 by Gray, Keeley & Seale, published by TPC 1978